SWEET DREAMS
BEDROOMS

SWEET DREAMS BEDROOMS

by Donna Dewberry

Furniture and Accessories by Jeff McWilliams

So Beautiful • So Easy • So Plaid™

© 2002 Plaid Enterprises, Inc.
Norcross, GA 30091-7600

www.plaidonline.com
800/842-4197 1/02
Printed in U.S.A.

ISBN: 1-55895-018-4

Dedication

To my husband, Marc. He has always pushed me to think "out of the box" and made me have vision through his belief that I could do anything, and always expecting me to just do it! I do enjoy seeing the finished product, to stand back and say WOW! I can do it! Marc always says not to look at the overwhelming task and feel like I will never get it done, but to work one step at a time. All this encouragement has helped me to be more than I could ever believe.

I want him to know I love and appreciate that he has been a large part of my dreams coming true and I will eternally be grateful for that.

Love,
Donna

DONNA DEWBERRY

Donna is the mother of seven children (four daughters and three sons) and a native Floridian. She has been involved with arts and crafts all her married life – over 25 years. After many evenings at her dining room table enjoying the pleasures of decorative painting, she developed a technique for stress-free painting that is the basis for her "One Stroke" series of painting books.

Donna finds peace and great pleasure in painting at her table – the same table where her children have shared their concerns or excitement about the day's activities, where she has conversed with friends and neighbors, where tears of frustration have been shed, where laughter and excitement have been exclaimed. Donna's creativity seems to shine brighter at this table.

One Stroke Certification

For information on Donna's three-and-a-half-day seminar, where she teaches her painting techniques as well as how to start a business in decorative painting and provides tips for being a good teacher, how to demo in stores, and how to get your painting published, contact her one of these ways:

• *By mail:*
Dewberry Designs
124 Robin Road
Altamonte Springs, FL 32701
• *By phone:*
407-260-2508
• *By fax:*
407-831-0658
• *On the Web:*
www.onestroke.com (certification and seminar information)
www.thestrokingedge.com (complete One Stroke resource)
• *By e-mail:*
email@onestroke.com

Special Thanks

I have a great many people to thank for the hard work in this book!

• Jeff McWilliams who had such vision as we created room by room with his never-ending ability to create another piece of furniture. Also, for the photo styling he did to give that "complete room" look we wanted. Thanks for sharing your talents with us, Jeff.

• Aleshia and George Dwayne and their children for sharing their home with us.

• Renee, Darren and Samantha Himmelbaum for letting me take over their home for weeks!

• Carol Smith for sharing her home and creative ideas throughout this project.

• My staff and Mickey Baskett for making the rest of this book happen.

Thanks,
Donna

CONTENTS

Complete Room Coordination with One Stroke™ Painting

From walls to floorcloths to furniture pieces and lamps, a room can become a beautiful artistic composition to live inside of, with simple One Stroke decorative painting. This book provides designs for nine rooms, 47 projects, including a style for every taste and every family member. There are guest rooms, nursery, boy's room, girl's room, master bedrooms.

Walls feature painted borders, murals, and/or all-over designs, some enhanced with coordinated painted wood cutouts for a dimensional effect. Painted floorcloths are cut to special shapes from the theme. Furniture pieces range from chests and desks to chairs and clothes hanging boards or posts to a blanket chest. Accessories like framed mirrors, photo frames, small shelves or painted bedspread and more embellish each room.

This big book will guide you through the quick and easy One Stroke painting technique and through the designs that create a dream room.

PAINTING SUPPLIES

Acrylic Paints

For all decorative painting, acrylic paints give great results. They dry quickly, are odor free, are easy to use, and come in a wide variety of colors. Plaid Enterprises manufactures the FolkArt® brand of acrylic paints that I use in all my decorative painting.

FolkArt® Acrylic Colors are high quality bottle acrylic paints. Their rich and creamy formulation and long open time make them perfect for decorative painting. They are offered in a huge range of wonderful, pre-mixed colors and in gleaming metallic shades. Cleanup is easy with soap and water.

FolkArt® Artists' Pigments™ are pure colors that are perfect for mixing your own shades. Their intense colors and creamy consistency are wonderful for blending, shading, and highlighting.

FolkArt® Sparkles™ are paints that add subtle iridescence or bright shimmer. They are available in a variety of bright and subtle colors.

Because FolkArt® paints are acrylic-based, cleanup is easy with soap and water.

Painting Mediums

FolkArt® Floating Medium 868 helps paint flow more smoothly, thus aiding your brush strokes.

FolkArt® Glass & Tile Medium 869 gives more tooth to non-porous surfaces and increases the durability of paint on glass, tile, and tin. Use it to undercoat the design (unless you're painting on etched glass; then an undercoat isn't necessary) and as a sealer.

FolkArt® Textile Medium 794 is mixed with paints when painting on fabric. It enables the paint to bond with the fibers of the fabric for durability and washability.

Painting Brushes

FolkArt® One Stroke™ Brushes have been developed especially for my painting technique. With the easy One Stroke™ techniques, you will need only a few specially designed brushes.

Large-size Brushes:
Specially made for painting large designs on furniture and walls.
1" flat 1184
1-1/2" flat 1189
Large Scruffy Brush 1190

Mid-size Brushes:
3/4" flat 1176
Scruffy Brush 1172
Brush Set 1171 includes a 3/4" flat, #12 flat, and #2 script liner. Brush Set #1177 includes a #8 flat and a #10 flat.

Mini Brushes:
Mini Scruffy Brush 1174
Mini Set 1173 includes a #6 flat, a #2 flat, and a #1 script liner.

Reusable Teaching Guides *Optional*

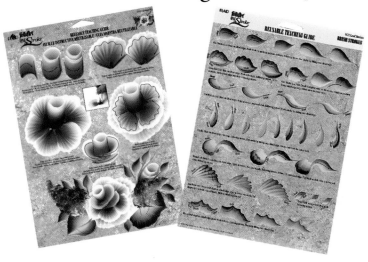

These are sold where you find other One Stroke painting supplies. Use these unique laminated worksheets to practice your strokes. To learn and practice, paint right on top of the illustrations and follow the strokes, then wipe clean and paint again! The *blank* Reusable Teaching Guide is a great way to practice once you've mastered the strokes with the illustrated guides.

You can also lay plastic sheets over the worksheets in this book and practice the strokes on the sheets.

Miscellaneous Supplies

Tracing paper, for tracing patterns from the pattern sheet

Transfer paper, black and white, and **stylus**, for transferring patterns

Brush Plus® Brush Cleaner, for cleaning brushes

Brush Basin®, for rinsing brushes

Paper towels, for blotting brushes

Sandpaper, to prepare wood

Finishes for Your Project

Let all painted projects dry 48 hours, then apply a finishing sealer or varnish to your painted projects to protect your beautiful painting and add sheen to the surface. I like clear, non-yellowing spray sealers best.

FolkArt® ClearCote™ Matte Acrylic Sealer 789: I use this when I want a matte finish.

FolkArt® ClearCote™ Hi-Shine Glaze 785: I use this for a glossy finish. (A spray sealer is especially suitable for metal surfaces, to eliminate the chance of streaking.)

FolkArt® Artist's Varnish 882-890: can be used on wood and other porous surfaces when a brush-on waterbase varnish is desired. Artist's Varnish is available in 2 oz., 4 oz., and 8 oz. bottles in gloss, satin, and matte sheens.

FolkArt® Glass & Tile Medium 869: is used to seal designs painted on glass.

Surfaces for Painting

Designs that use the One Stroke™ technique can be painted on wood, metal, fabric, walls, canvas, and glass. Specific surfaces used for the projects in this book are described in the individual project instructions, and sources are listed. You can also cut some of the smaller accessories from wood using the patterns given in this book. Many of the wood projects are made by *Jeff McWilliams*. You may find similar items at crafts or department stores.

About Jeff McWilliams

Jeff is well known for his beautiful set designs, trade booth designs and furniture creations. He has created two lines of furniture "The DRY GRASS Collection" and "The Birdhouse Bedroom Collection." Jeff McWilliams has a design studio in Norcross, Georgia, where he is involved in a variety of unique design projects. Jeff has authored his own book, entitled *Flea Market Finds*, published by Plaid Enterprises, Inc., as well as contributed to several books with Donna Dewberry, *The Birdhouse Bedroom* and *Furniture Fantasy*.

Furniture and accessories in book available from J.M. Original Creations, 5965 Peachtree Corners East, Suite A-3, Norcross, GA 30071, Phone 770-248-9010. Web address: www.jmoriginalcreations.com ❏

GENERAL INSTRUCTIONS

Using One Stroke™ Brushes

One Stroke brushes are essential for the One Stroke technique. They have been designed especially for this type of stroke work. Here's a brief explanation on the use and purpose of each brush:

Scruffy:

I originally created the scruffy by shaping the bristles of an old, worn out brush into an oval after carefully cutting them to a uniform length of about 1/2". The One Stroke scruffy brushes you can buy are ready to use. All you have to do is "fluff the scruff" – remove the brush from the packaging and form the bristles into an oval shape by gently pulling them, then twist the bristles in the palm of your hand until they are a nice oval shape. Now you're ready to pounce the brush into paint and begin.

Continued on next page

A fluffed scruffy brush is used to paint mosses, wisteria, lilacs, and some hair and fur, faux finishes, and shading textures. This brush is not used with water. To clean, pounce the bristles in the Brush Basin® – don't rake them; the natural bristles can break. Allow the brush to dry thoroughly before painting with it again.

Flat Brushes:

#2, #4, #6, #8, #10, #12, 3/4", 1", and 1-1/2"

One Stroke flat brushes are designed with longer bristles and less thickness in the body of the brush than other flat brushes, so they have a much sharper chisel edge. A sharp chisel edge is essential as most of strokes begin and then end on the chisel edge.

These brushes are ready to use from the package. Simply dampen the bristles in water and dry them with a paper towel before loading. When cleaning flat brushes, you can use the rake in the bottom of the Brush Basin®. Flat One Stroke brushes are synthetic and don't have a tendency to break, but be gentle.

Remember everyone's comfort zone is different. While one painter is comfortable using a #10, another painter may be just as comfortable with a 3/4" flat brush. Use the size brush that is suitable for the size of your project and with which you feel most comfortable.

Script liners:

Two sizes, #2 and #1

- The #1 script liner (sometimes referred to as the mini) is used for small detail work where a lot of control is needed.
- The #2 script liner is used where less control is needed, such as when painting curlicues or string ribbons.

They are used with paint that is inky (thinned with water to the consistency of ink.) Use them this way: Wet the brush. Load paint on your palette. Dip the brush in water three to four times. Roll the wet brush in the paint, twirling the brush to load. Pull out to the side of the palette until well loaded with inky paint.

Loading One Stroke™ Brushes

If You're a Left-Handed Painter

- Always start where I say to end and end your stroke where I indicate to start.
- When you are stroking leaves, turn your practice sheets or worksheets so you stroke the tip of the leaf towards your body.

Clean script liners as you would flats; be gentle, but clean thoroughly.

Loading One Stroke™ Brushes

1. Wet your brush and gently tap on paper towel to remove excess water.
2. Pick up paint by dipping one corner of the brush in one color and the opposite corner of the brush in another color (for double loading).
3. Stroke brush back and forth in a sweeping motion. Repeat step once or twice until the brush is full of paint two-thirds of the way up the bristles.
- When brush is loaded correctly, your strokes should feel as though the bristles glide. If the brush is coarse or splits, you do not have enough paint on the brush.
- *Don't* brush back and forth on your palette every time you pick up paint – if you do, you won't have enough paint on your brush to finish your strokes.
- When loading brushes #6 and smaller, load with one color first, then sidestroke into the second color to double load.
- When you run out of paint and need to reload, pick up a touch of paint of either color and start painting.

Using Floating Medium in the One Stroke™ Technique

Rather than following the bottle instructions, use Floating Medium this way to help the paint flow more smoothly:

1. Squeeze a puddle of Floating Medium on your palette.
2. Load brush with paint first, as instructed.
3. Dip the tips of the bristles of the loaded brush straight down in the puddle of Floating Medium.
4. Stroke the brush on the palette two or three times, and you're ready to paint.

Transferring Patterns

When using the One Stroke painting technique you may not need a pattern to paint the designs. The brushes are the size you will need to make the strokes for the designs, eliminating the need for patterns. However, if you feel you need some patterns, we have given line drawings of the designs on pages following the instructions for each bedroom. The designs for the projects in this book are very large, therefore, most of the patterns could not be given actual size. An enlargement size is given with the pattern. Take the pattern to a copy shop or a blue print shop if you need to have them enlarged.

Tips for transferring patterns:

• Reduce or enlarge the patterns as necessary on a copy machine to accommodate the size of your project.
• Use dark transfer paper for light surfaces and white for dark surfaces.
• Lightly tape the pattern to the surface to keep it from sliding.
• It is not necessary to trace every fine detail. Transfer the main outlines of the pattern. Tracing every detail takes away from the natural look you are trying to attain.

To Transfer a Pattern to a Wall or Piece of Furniture

The designs in this book can be enlarged and painted on walls or furniture. Here's how:

1. Trace or transfer the pattern to graph paper. *Tip:* Use a copy machine to copy the pattern on graph paper.
2. Draw a grid on the wall or piece of furniture where you are planning to place the design.
3. Use a pencil to lightly sketch the design on the surface, using the pattern on the graph paper as your guide.

Painting Large Objects

When painting on walls or large pieces of furniture many times a brush is not big enough to basecoat an area or of an appropriate texture for painting an object. Here are some tips for painting large areas:

• **Using a Sponge for Basecoating:** A household sponge is a wonderful tool to use to apply a basecoat of color to a large design. Dampen the sponge with water and squeeze out the excess water. Load the entire sponge with color. You can pick up more than one color on the sponge. Rub the surface of the area in a circular motion to fill the area with paint.

• **Painting Shapes:** The sponge can also be used to paint shapes; such as a large flower pot or a vase on a wall. First, load the entire dampened sponge with the color that is predominant. Then stroke the edge of the sponge into the shading color. Place the sponge on the surface, and use the edge of the sponge like a pencil to draw the shape of the element, adding pressure on the edge with your fingers as you move the sponge along. I like to use this method also when I am painting creases in clothing or folds in a body.

• **Using a Sea Sponge:** This is a wonderful tool to use to paint fluffy clouds by using it in a pouncing motion. It can also be multi-loaded with color to paint areas of moss.

• **Painted Walls:** If walls are painted with flat paint, it is sometimes difficult for the brush to move and glide on this finish. You may need to work some water (very little) into loaded brush occasionally the help the brush move. If too much water is added, you will lose your shading and the paint will become muddy. A paint with a satin or eggshell finish is recommended for the walls and larger painting surfaces.

Sponged Finish Tips

Follow these steps when you're sponging a faux finish. Using a sponge is similar to using a scruffy brush – if you *over-pounce*, you will muddy up the look. You want the colors to be distinct. (On a small project, you could use a scruffy brush instead of a sponge.)

1. Squeeze paint colors on your palette as directed.
2. Dampen a household sponge in water, squeeze dry.
3. Pounce half the sponge in one color and the other half in the second color.
4. Pounce the sponge on the surface, remembering to vary the placement of the sponge so as not to create a repeated pattern.
5. Re-load sponge as it begins to lose its color.

DAISIES & BUTTERFLIES

GATHER THESE SUPPLIES

FolkArt® Acrylic Colors:
Basil Green 645
Berry Wine 434
Dark Plum 469
Grass Green 644
Raspberry Wine 935
School Bus Yellow 736
Sunflower 432
Thicket 924
Wicker White 901

FolkArt® Artists' Pigment™ Colors:
Burnt Umber 462
Raw Umber 485

Yellow Light 918

FolkArt® One Stroke™ Brushes:
Flats – sizes #12, 3/4" and 1"
Script liner – size #2
Scruffy brush

Painting Surfaces:
• Pre-painted Walls (it is best to use egg-shell finish latex paint as a base for your decorative painting. This room started with lavender walls.
• Vinyl flooring for floorcloth, 36" x 48" (You will use the backside of vinyl flooring to paint floorcloth. Canvas can also be used to make floorcloth.)
• Wood bench*
• Bumblebee lamp with white shade*
• Wood daisy table*
• Wood window pots mirror frame*
• Wood butterfly birdhouse*
• Two wood ladybug peg hanging boards*
*(www.jmoriginalcreations.com)

Other Supplies:
FolkArt® One Stroke™ Sponge Painters 1195
FolkArt® Floating Medium 868
Sponge

Painted Wall Designs

PREPARATION
Transfer patterns to walls.

PAINT THE DESIGN

Background Foliage for Border:
1. Dampen sponge and dip into Basil Green and Wicker White. Rub onto surface in a circular motion.
2. While paint is damp, pick up fresh paint and pounce over rubbed color to create the faux finish background.

Leaves & Vines on Border:
Refer to "Leaves & Cattail" and "Branch/ Vines, Seaweed, Waterlily & Frog" Painting Worksheets, using colors given below.
1. Double load the 1" flat brush with Thicket and Wicker White. Add a touch of Sunflower to the white side. Paint vines with the chisel edge of brush. Vines should not be too tight.
2. Add a few more vines coming off of main vine to fill in.
3. With same brush, paint full leaves by pushing, wiggling, and sliding back up to tip. Repeat on other side for some leaves. For others, push and slide on one side. As soon as you paint a leaf, pull the stem into it from the vine.
4. With the 1" flat brush, add some One Stroke leaves by pushing, then

turning as you lift back up to the chisel. Add stems. Paint these in little groups.
5. Load the #12 flat brush with Thicket and paint some groups of smaller One Stroke leaves.

Daisies:
Refer to "Flowers" Painting Worksheet #2, using colors given below.
1. Load the 1" flat brush with Wicker White. Start on outside of petal, on chisel edge, and push as you lean and pull towards the center, lifting brush up to chisel at end. Paint daisies on foliage in clusters as seen in the photo of project.
2. Load the scruffy brush by pouncing into Yellow Light. Sideload a little Raw Umber onto one side. Pounce on the daisy centers.
3. Add the daisies on wall above the daisy border in the same manner.

Wisteria:
Refer to "Feather, Moss & Wisteria" Painting Worksheet, using colors given below.
Double load the scruffy brush by pouncing half into Wicker White and half into Dark Plum. Pounce on the wisteria. Taper end by leaning onto one side of the brush.

Butterflies:
Refer to "Critters" Painting Worksheet, using colors given below.
1. With a small sponge painter, base-coat wings with Raspberry Sherbert. Load the 3/4" flat with Floating Medium. Sideload into Berry Wine. Add shading to butterfly. Other color variations include Wicker White with Dark Plum and Wicker White with School Bus Yellow.
2. Double load the #12 flat brush with School Bus Yellow and Wicker White. Paint spots on butterflies with yellow side of brush turned outward. (Yellow butterfly has Dark Plum with Wicker White.)
3. To paint bodies, double load the 3/4" flat brush with Thicket and Yellow Light with some Wicker White. Start at head and begin on chisel edge of brush, then push down and pull, overlapping strokes slightly and making them smaller each time. Use chisel edge to paint tail.
4. Dip handle end of brush into Burnt Umber and dot on tips of antennae.
5. Load inky Burnt Umber onto the #2 script liner. Paint outlines and antennae.

Continued on page 14

12

Continued from page 12
Ladybugs:
Refer to "Critters" Painting Worksheet, using colors given below.
1. With sponge painter, basecoat with Raspberry Wine.
2. Load the 3/4" flat brush with Berry Wine and paint heads.
3. Load the 3/4" flat brush with Floating Medium and sideload into the Berry Wine. Add shading to ladybugs.

4. Double load the #12 flat brush with Thicket and Basil Green. Paint spots with Thicket side of brush outward.
5. On chisel edge of brush and leading with Thicket, paint stripes on tails.
6. Load the #12 flat brush with Floating Medium and sideload into Wicker White. Add highlight on heads.
7. Load the #2 script liner with inky Burnt Umber. Add outlines as in photo of project.

Dragonflies:
Refer to "Critters" Painting Worksheet, using colors given below.
1. Load the 1" flat brush with Floating Medium. Sideload into Wicker White. With white side outward, paint outer edges of wings, then brush back and forth to fill in centers.
2. Paint bodies the same as butterflies, using Grass Green and Thicket.
3. Outline with inky Burnt Umber on #2 script liner.

Large Bees:
Refer to "Critters" Painting Worksheet, using colors given below.
1. Using sponge painter, basecoat with Sunflower.
2. Load the 3/4" flat brush with Floating Medium and sideload into School Bus Yellow. Add shading.
3. Load the 1" flat brush with Floating Medium. Sideload into Wicker White. With white side outward, paint outer edges of wings, then brush back and forth to fill in centers.
4. Double load the 1" flat brush with Burnt Umber and Wicker White. With Burnt Umber side outward paint the heads.
5. Load the #2 script liner with Burnt Umber that is only a little inky. Paint lines, tails, outlines, and eyes. With paint that is a little inkier, paint mouths, eyebrows and wing outlines. ❑

Garden-Style Bench

PREPARATION
1. Lightly sand wood and clean it off.
2. Basecoat with two coats of Wicker White (or equivalent color wall paint). Allow to dry.
3. Transfer patterns to bench where needed. Refer to photo of projects for placement.

PAINT THE DESIGN
Paint background foliage, vines and leaves, daisies, wisteria, and butterfly by same instructions given for walls. ❑

15

Daisy Floorcloth

PREPARATION

1. Cut daisy floorcloth from vinyl flooring by pattern.
2. Basecoat backside of vinyl with two coats of Wicker White (or equivalent color wall paint). Allow to dry.
3. Transfer parts of pattern you feel you might need. (Transfer butterfly after daisies are painted.)

PAINT THE DESIGN

Daisies:

1. Load the 1" flat brush with Floating Medium. Sideload Yellow Light and add shading in middle of daisy petals. Use more yellow for the darkest yellow daisy.
2. CENTERS: Load a sponge painter with Yellow Light and some Floating Medium, if needed, and basecoat centers. Double load the scruffy brush with Yellow Light and Raw Umber. Pounce on shading as seen in photo of project.
3. With inky Burnt Umber on #2 script liner, paint outlines on daisies.

Butterfly:

1. When daisies are dry, transfer butterfly.
2. Paint butterfly by instructions given for walls. □

Daisy Table

PREPARATION

1. Lightly sand wood and clean it off.
2. Basecoat with two coats of Wicker White (or equivalent color wall paint). Allow to dry.
3. Transfer pattern lines where needed. Refer to photo of projects for placement.

PAINT THE DESIGN

Stems & Leaves:

1. Use a sponge to basecoat with Basil Green and Floating Medium for long smooth strokes.

16

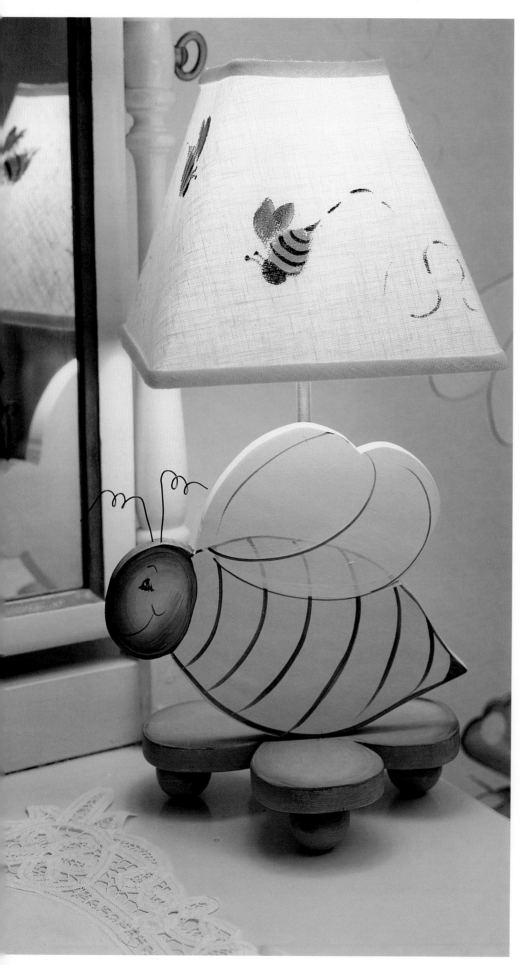

2. Load the 1" flat brush with Floating Medium. Sideload with Thicket. Add shading.

Daisies:
Paint according to instructions given for Floorcloth. ❏

Bumblebee Lamp

PREPARATION

1. Lightly sand wood and clean it off.
2. Basecoat with two coats of Wicker White. Allow to dry.
3. Use a sponge painter to basecoat with Basil Green and Floating Medium for long smooth strokes and paint the rim and ball feet.
4. Transfer parts of bee pattern needed. Transfer small bee pattern to lamp shade.

PAINT THE DESIGN

Large Bee:
Paint by instructions given for bee on walls.

Small Bee:
Refer to "Critters" Painting Worksheet, using colors given below.

1. Use the scruffy brush to pounce School Bus Yellow bee bodies.
2. Double load the #12 flat brush with mostly Wicker White and a little Burnt Umber. Start at outer end of wing, on chisel edge of brush, lean and push, then pull back up to the chisel edge at body.
3. Load the #12 flat brush with Burnt Umber. Paint heads.
4. With inky Burnt Umber on the #2 script liner, paint stripes, antennae, and flight lines. ❏

Butterfly Birdhouse

PREPARATION

1. Lightly sand wood and clean it off.
2. Basecoat with two coats of Wicker White. Allow to dry.

PAINT THE DESIGN

1. Re-basecoat ball legs with School Bus Yellow, house and base with Sunflower, and roof and perches with Grass Green. Allow to dry.
2. Wash on School Bus Yellow and Floating Medium with a sponge painter.
3. Load the 3/4" flat brush with Floating Medium. Sideload Grass Green and paint shading on wings.
4. Load the #2 script liner with inky Burnt Umber and paint wing details. ❏

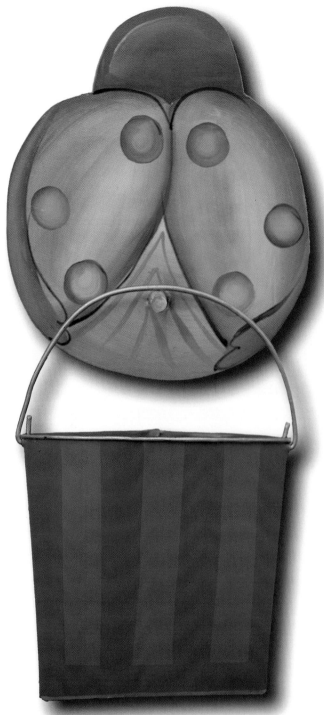

Ladybug Peg Hanger Board

PREPARATION

1. Lightly sand wood and clean it off.
2. Basecoat with two coats of Wicker White. Allow to dry.

PAINT THE DESIGN

Paint by instructions given for ladybugs on walls. ❏

Window Pots Mirror

PREPARATION

1. Lightly sand wood and clean it off.
2. Basecoat with two coats of Wicker White (or equivalent color wall paint). Allow to dry.
3. Transfer pattern lines where needed. Refer to photo of projects for placement.

PAINT THE DESIGN

Stems, Leaves & Pots:

1. Use a sponge to basecoat with Basil Green and Floating Medium for long smooth strokes. Use a lighter, more transparent shade (more Floating Medium, less Basil Green) on pots than on stems and leaves.
2. Load the 1" flat brush with Floating Medium. Sideload with Thicket. Add shading.
3. Load the scruffy brush with Thicket and Yellow Light and pounce on moss.

Daisies:

1. Load the 1" flat brush with Floating Medium. Sideload Yellow Light and add shading in middle of daisy petals.
2. Load the scruffy brush with Yellow Light. Pounce an edge into Raw Umber. Pounce on daisy centers. Refer to photo of project for shading placement. ❑

Patterns

Enlarge Patterns at % given or to size needed.

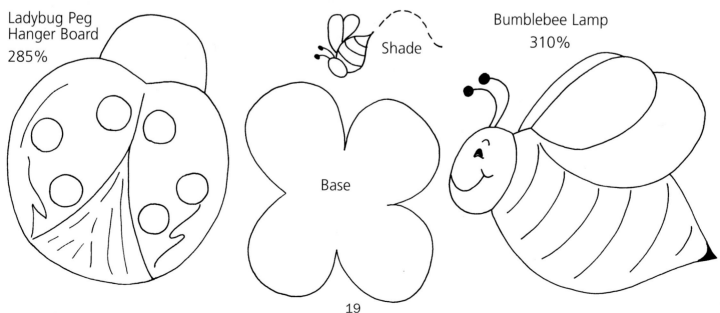

Ladybug Peg
Hanger Board
285%

Shade

Bumblebee Lamp
310%

Base

Patterns

Enlarge Patterns at % given or to size needed.

Daisy Floorcloth:
Use photo as a guide to create pattern with daisy design.
350%

Daisy
Table
Top
350%

Daisy Table Base
500%

Garden Style
Bench Seat
310%

20

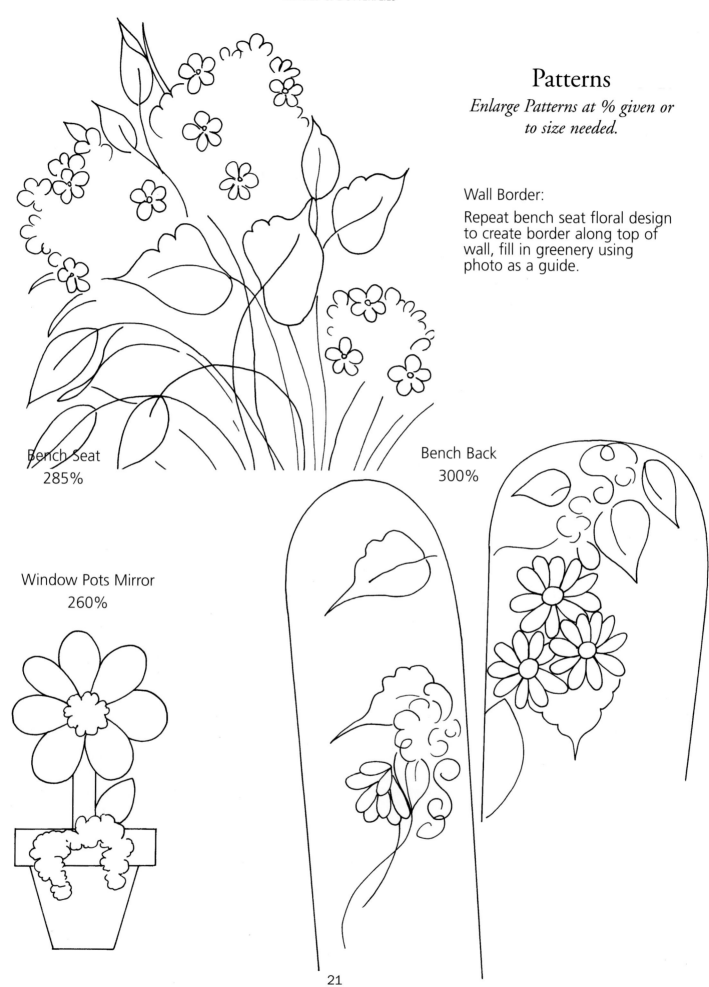

Patterns

Enlarge Patterns at % given or to size needed.

Wall Border:

Repeat bench seat floral design to create border along top of wall, fill in greenery using photo as a guide.

Bench Seat
285%

Bench Back
300%

Window Pots Mirror
260%

21

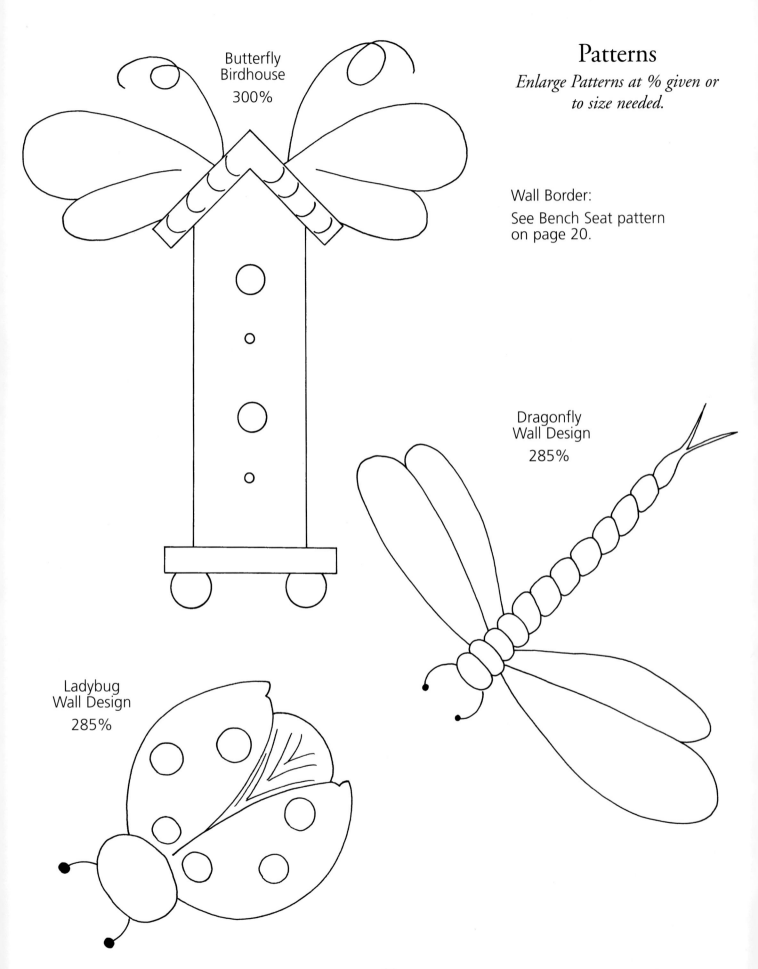

Butterfly
Birdhouse
300%

Patterns

*Enlarge Patterns at % given or
to size needed.*

Wall Border:
See Bench Seat pattern
on page 20.

Dragonfly
Wall Design
285%

Ladybug
Wall Design
285%

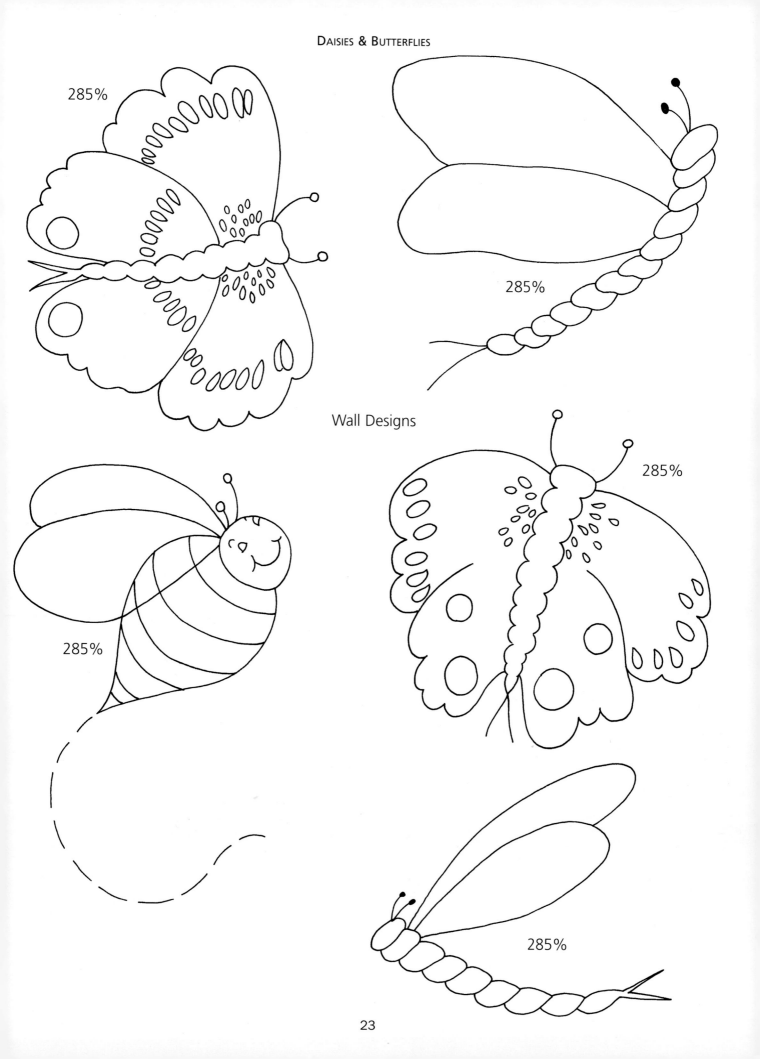

285%

285%

Wall Designs

285%

285%

285%

23

By the Pond

GATHER THESE SUPPLIES

FolkArt® Acrylic Colors:
Berry Wine 434
Butter Pecan 939
Engine Red 436
Grass Green 644
Green Forest 448
Licorice 938
Maple Syrup 945
Midnight 964
School Bus Yellow 736
Thicket 924
Wicker White 901

FolkArt® Artists' Pigment™ Colors:
Brilliant Ultramarine 484
Burnt Sienna 943
Burnt Umber 462

FolkArt® One Stroke™ Brushes:
Flats – sizes #12, 3/4", 1",
and 1-1/2"
Script liner – size #2
Scruffy brush

Painting Surface:
• Pre-painted Walls (It is
  recommended that you paint
  your walls with satin or eggshell
  finish paint. This one started
  off-white.)
• Five wood paddle oars for headboard (These can be purchased
  at a sporting goods store where
  canoeing equipment is sold.)
• Vinyl flooring for floorcloth 36"
  x 48" (You will use the backside
  of vinyl flooring to paint
  floorcloth. Canvas can also be
  used to make floorcloth.)
• Wood cattail lamp*
• Wood turtle mirror*
• Wood frog cutouts*
• Wood fish chair*
• Wood chest with fish drawer
  pulls*
* www.jmoriginalcreations.com

Other Supplies:
FolkArt® One Stroke™ Sponge
Painters 1195
FolkArt® Floating Medium 868
FolkArt® ClearCote™ Matte
Acrylic Sealer 789
Household Sponge

Painted Wall Designs

PREPARATION

1. Lightly pencil the outline of the area of the water on the walls.
2. Transfer patterns to walls where needed. Refer to photos of projects for placement. (Some patterns will need to be added as you go along, as areas under some items will be painted first.)

PAINT THE DESIGN

Grass & Cattails:

Refer to "Leaves & Cattail" Painting Worksheet, using colors given below.

1. For blades, double load the 1-1/2" flat brush with Grass Green and Green Forest, then work in Floating Medium. Paint tall grass blades around the room, varying heights of the grass blades.
2. For cattail stalks, double load the 1-1/2" flat brush with Grass Green and Green Forest, then work in Floating Medium. On the chisel edge of the brush, pull stalks for the cattails down into the grass. Remember to vary the heights of the stalks.
3. Load the scruffy brush with Burnt Sienna and Maple Syrup. Pounce the cattails, keeping the darker color on one side.
4. With the same loaded brush, pick up a little School Bus Yellow and pounce a highlight on the top edge of each cattail.
5. Using the chisel edge of a 3/4" flat brush, pull a short stalk out of the top of each cattail.
6. Load the 1-1/2" flat brush with Grass Green and Green Forest, then work in Floating Medium. On the chisel edge, pull a thin blade of grass from the main stalk, like a calyx, up and past the lower part of each cattail.

Dragonflies:

Refer to "Critters" Painting Worksheet, using colors given below.

1. WINGS: Load the 3/4" flat brush with Wicker White and add Floating Medium. To paint wings, start on the chisel edge and stroke out toward the end of the wing. Stroking out toward the edges, push down to spread the bristles. Pull back to finish the other side of the wing and slide back to the chisel. If the wall you are painting on is very white, you can pick up a little bit of Licorice to make a gray shadow so the wings will show.
2. BODY: Double load a #12 flat brush with Thicket and Green Forest. With the Green Forest to the outside, paint a half circle for the head. Paint each body segment by starting on the chisel edge with the Green Forest turned upward, and push and pull. Keep the Green Forest up on each body segment. Use the chisel edge of the brush to pull the forked tail.
3. ANTENNAE: Use a script liner and water to make an inky puddle of Thicket. Roll the bristles in the puddle and pull out to a point. Then on the tip of the bristles, touch and pull antennae to the head.

Wall Pond:

1. Moisten a sponge. Stroke into Brilliant Ultramarine and pick up a little Wicker White on one side of the sponge. Outline the edge of the pond with the blue against the penciled line and use the sponge to fill in the pond area. If the water is too blue, pick up more white. If it is too pale, add more Brilliant Ultramarine. Let dry.
2. Load the 1-1/2" flat brush with Floating Medium, then sideload with Wicker White. Paint the waves on the pond. Refer to photo of project.

Alligator:

1. Pencil or transfer the shape of the alligator, lily pads, and water lilies.
2. Moisten a sponge and stroke into the Grass Green. Add a little Green Forest to one side. Outline the alligator and fill in with the sponge.
3. Double load a 3/4" flat brush with Floating Medium and Green Forest. Paint outline and details.
4. Add a lot more Floating Medium and paint the waterline on the alligator.
5. ALLIGATOR'S EYE: Load the 3/4" flat brush with Wicker White and paint the circle for the eyeball. Load the #12 flat brush with Licorice and paint iris. Double load the 3/4" flat brush with Grass Green and Green Forest. Paint upper lid. Load the #2 script liner with inky Licorice and outline the eye. Load the #2 script liner with inky Wicker White and paint a highlight across the eyeball.
6. TEETH: Load the #12 brush with Grass Green and sideload with Wicker White. Paint each tooth, using the same stroke as you would for a One Stroke leaf.

Lily Pads:

Refer to "Branch/Vines, Seaweed, Waterlily & Frog" Painting Worksheet, using colors given below.

1. Moisten sponge painter and stroke into Grass Green. Add a little Green Forest to one side. Outline each lily pad and fill in with the sponge.
2. Load the 3/4" flat brush with Floating Medium and sideload with Green Forest. Paint outlining and details. Stroke veins on with the chisel edge of the brush.

Frog:

Refer to "Branch/Vines, Seaweed, Waterlily & Frog" Painting Worksheet, using colors given below.

1. Transfer frog on top of the lily pad.
2. Use a moistened sponge painter dipped in Grass Green to fill in the frog.
3. Load a #12 flat brush with Grass Green and paint tongue.
4. Double load the #12 flat brush with Grass Green and Green Forest. Add details.
5. EYE: Load the #12 flat brush with Wicker White and paint the circle for the eyeball. Load the #12 flat brush with Licorice and paint the iris of the eye. Dip the handle end of brush into Wicker White and dot highlights on the iris. Double load the #12 flat brush with Grass Green and Green Forest. Paint upper lid. Load the #2 script liner with inky Licorice and outline the eye.

26

Dragonfly:

Refer to "Critters" Painting Worksheet, using colors given below.

1. Load the #12 flat brush with Wicker White and paint wings of the dragonfly at the end of the frog's tongue. Pull from the outside of the wing toward the body.

2. Paint the body with a #12 flat brush double loaded with Grass Green and Thicket.

3. Load the #2 script liner into inky Licorice. Using just the tip, touch and pull antennae to the head. You can also detail the wings of the fly with the same script liner and inky Licorice.

Waterlilies:

Refer to "Branch/Vines, Seaweed, Waterlily & Frog" Painting Worksheet, using colors given below.

Load the 3/4" flat brush with Wicker White and pick up a little Floating Medium. Paint lily petals starting at the back of the flower. Starting on the chisel edge, push down, slide brush up to the chisel and slide back down the other side. Occasionally add a little Maple Syrup to one side of the brush for depth. □

Paddle Headboard

The tips of the paddles are "color-washed" with different colors of paint. Each paddle is painted to a different depth. Refer to photo of project.

1. Use a moistened sponge painter dipped in Midnight to paint two paddles.
2. Repeat with Engine Red to paint the other two paddles.
3. Paint the remaining paddle in the same manner using Green Forest.
4. Load the 1" flat brush with Midnight and paint a 1" band across the middle of the color-washed area on the Midnight paddle.
5. Load the 1" flat brush with Green Forest and paint a 1" band at the lower edge of the Green Forest color wash.
6. Using the same loaded brush on the chisel edge (same color), stroke a line at the base of all the color-washes.
7. When dry, spray oars lightly with matte acrylic sealer. ❑

Cattail Lamp

PREPARATION

1. Basecoat the lamp with Wicker White. Let dry. With a moistened sponge painter, color-wash lamp with Grass Green. Basecoat ball feet with Grass Green.

PAINT THE DESIGN

1. Double load a 3/4" flat brush with Green Forest and Grass Green and paint details on the lily pad base, the grass blades, and stalks of the cattails.
2. Load the 3/4" flat brush with Burnt Sienna and paint the cattails.
3. Load the scruffy brush with Burnt Sienna and Maple Syrup. With Maple Syrup to outer edge, pounce one side of the cattail and the tip. ❑

28

Pond Floorcloth

PREPARATION

1. Cut out vinyl flooring in the shape of the pond. On the backside of the vinyl, basecoat with Wicker White. Let dry.

PAINT THE DESIGN

Water:

1. Moisten a sponge painter. Stroke sponge into the Brilliant Ultramarine and pick up Wicker White on one edge. With the Brilliant Ultramarine side of the sponge to the outside edge of the rug, paint the water following the shape of the rug. Make tighter and tighter circles until the rug is filled in.
2. Double load the 1" flat brush with Wicker White and Floating Medium and paint the water ripples.

Lily pads:

Refer to "Branch/Vines, Seaweed, Waterlily & Frog" Painting Worksheet, using colors given below.

1. Transfer pattern of lily pads onto the rug.
2. With a moistened sponge painter dipped into Grass Green, paint the lily pads.
3. Double load a 3/4" flat brush with Green Forest and Floating Medium and add details. Stroke veins on the chisel edge of the brush.

30

Dragonflies:

Refer to "Critters" Painting Worksheet, using colors given below.

1. WINGS: Load the 3/4" brush flat with Wicker White and add Floating Medium. Start on the chisel edge and stroke out toward the ends of the wings. Stroke out toward the ends, pushing down to spread the bristles.

Pull back to finish the other side of the wing sliding back to the chisel.

2. BODY: Double load a #12 flat brush with Thicket and Green Forest. With Green Forest to the outside, paint a half circle for the head. Paint each body segment by starting on the chisel edge with Green Forest upward, push, and pull. Keep the Green Forest up on each body segment.

3. Use the chisel edge of the brush to pull the forked tail.

4. ANTENNAE: Use a #2 script liner and water to make an inky puddle of Thicket. Roll the bristles in the puddle and pull out to a point. On the tip of the bristles touch and pull antennae to the head.

Finish Floorcloth:

When dry, finish with matte acrylic sealer. ❑

Wood Frogs

Pictured on Floorcloth

PREPARATION

1. Use the 1" flat brush with Grass Green and basecoat frogs.

PAINT THE DESIGN

1. Double load the #12 flat brush with Green Forest and Floating Medium. Paint spots and other details.

2. Load the #12 flat brush with Wicker White and paint eyeballs. Load the #12 flat brush with Licorice and paint pupils. ❑

Turtle Mirror

PREPARATION

1. Basecoat the piece with Wicker White. Let dry. With a moistened sponge painter, color-wash with Grass Green.

PAINT THE DESIGN

1. Load a 1" flat brush with Burnt Sienna and paint the wide stripes on the life preserver.

2. Double load the 3/4" flat brush with Green Forest and Floating Medium and paint the details along the edges and the turtle eyes. ❑

Fish Chair

PREPARATION

1. Basecoat the chair with Wicker White. Let dry. Color-wash everything but the fish with Midnight.

PAINT THE DESIGN

Fish:

1. Load a moistened sponge painter with Butter Pecan and Floating Medium. Start at the bottom of the fish and stroke across and upward. Pick up some Berry Wine and work into the middle area of the fish. As you work up the fish, add Green Forest.

2. Double load the 3/4" flat brush with Green Forest and Floating Medium. Add shading on tail, top of fish, and on the fins. On the chisel edge of brush, paint the gills.

3. Dip handle end of brush into Butter Pecan and dot eye area, sliding the handle around to make dot big enough.

4. Wipe handle off, dip it into Licorice, and dot fish to make speckles. Also use the handle to dot the eye (pupil) black.

5. Use the script liner and Wicker White to add highlights to the eye.

Lure:

1. Load the #12 flat brush with Wicker White and basecoat the top of lure.

2. Load the #12 flat brush with Engine Red and paint the end of the lure.

3. Load the #2 script liner into inky Licorice and paint the hook and the fishing line, using just the tip of the bristles. Add stripe to the lure.

4. Double load #12 flat brush with Wicker White and Thicket. Using chisel edge, leading with Wicker White, paint feather on lure. ❏

32

Five Drawer Chest

PREPARATION

1. Basecoat the chest and bobbers with Wicker White. Let dry.
2. Color-wash everything except the drawer fronts and the bobbers with Midnight. Color-wash drawer fronts with Green Forest.

PAINT THE DESIGN

Bobbers:

Load the 3/4" flat brush with Engine Red and paint the bottoms and top dowels of bobbers.

Fish Drawer Pulls:

1. Load the #12 flat brush with Butter Pecan and Floating Medium. Paint fronts.
2. Add details using Floating Medium and Midnight or Floating Medium and Green Forest. Refer to photo of project.
3. Load the #2 script liner with Floating Medium and Engine Red to paint stripes.
4. Dip handle end of brush into Licorice and dot the eyes. Load the #2 script liner into inky Wicker White and paint highlights on eyes.
5. Load the #12 flat brush with Floating Medium and Maple Syrup. Paint edges of the fish.

Lettering:

1. Paint letters with Wicker White.
2. Outline letters on one side of each with Engine Red. ❏

Patterns

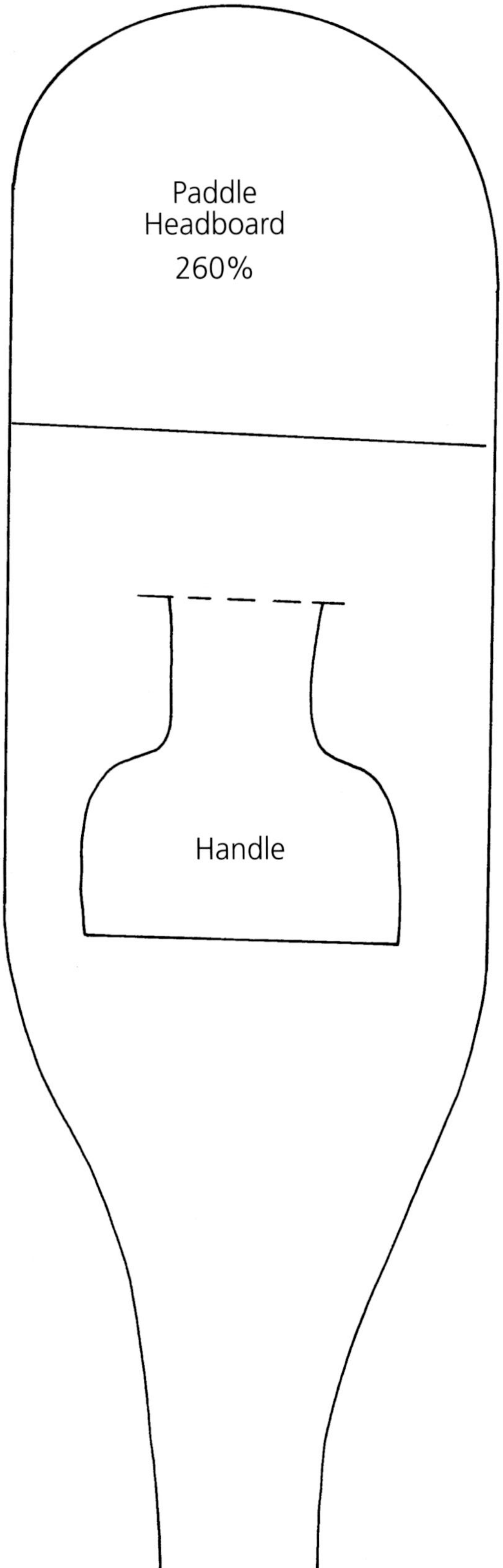

Paddle
Headboard
260%

Handle

Cattails
on Wall
465%

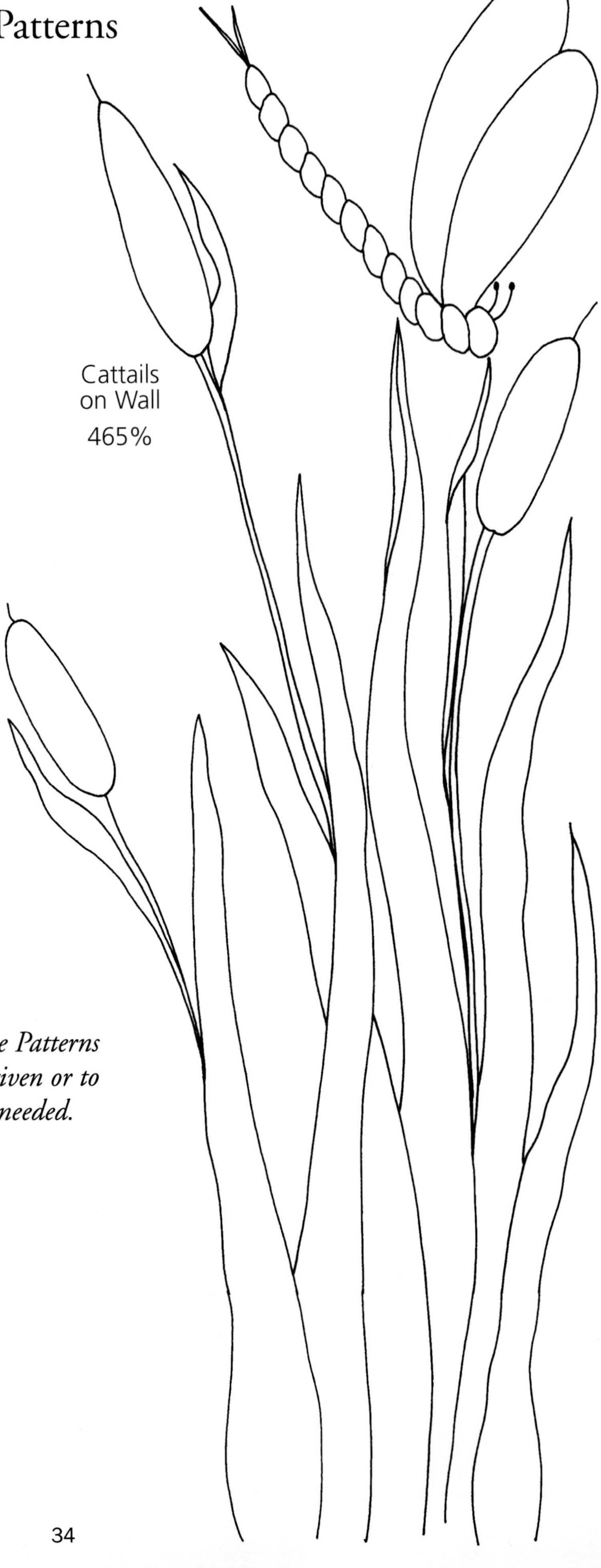

*Enlarge Patterns
at % given or to
size needed.*

Add 23"
from here to handle

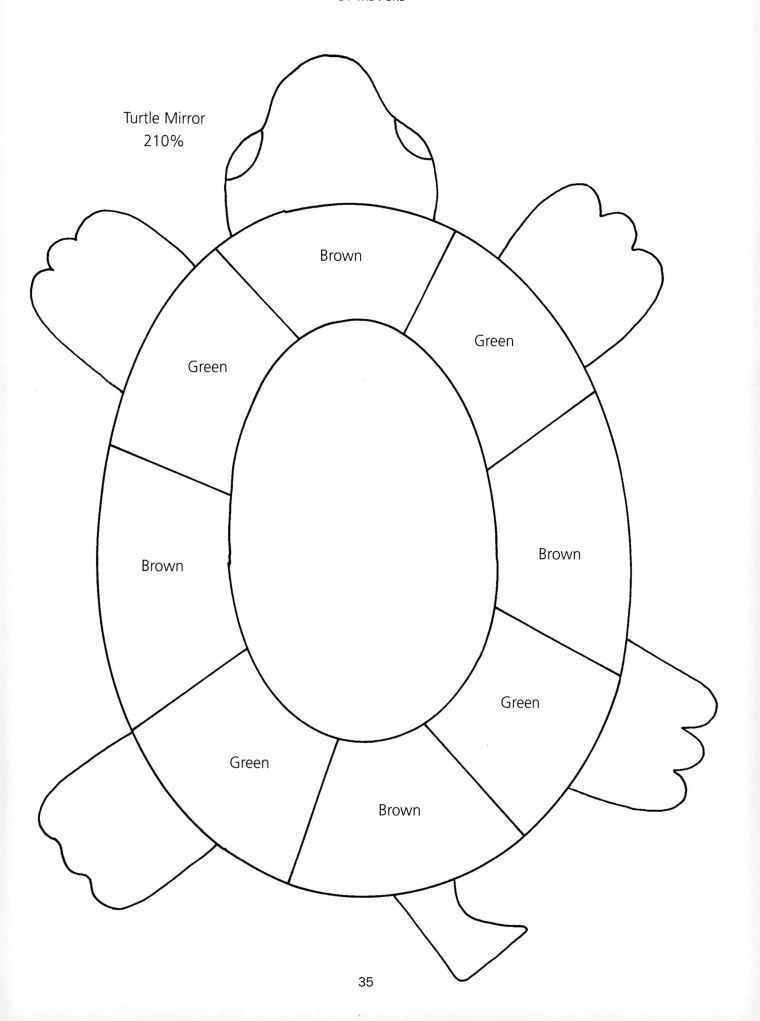

Turtle Mirror
210%

Brown

Green

Green

Brown

Brown

Green

Green

Brown

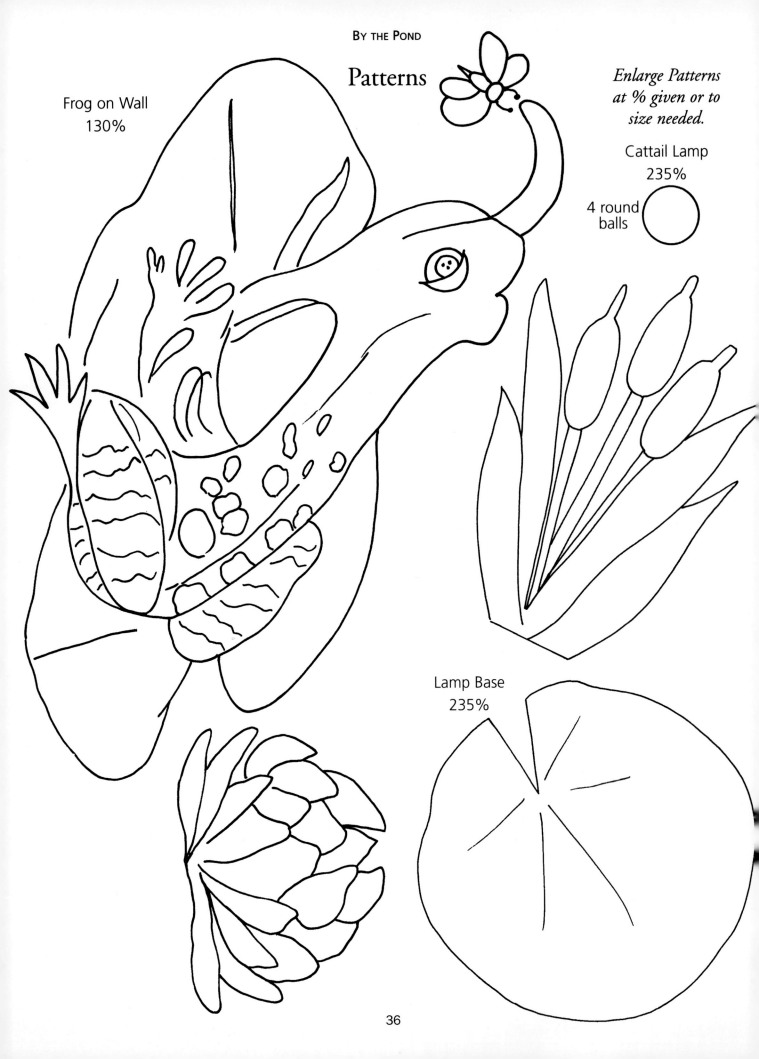

Patterns

Frog on Wall
130%

*Enlarge Patterns
at % given or to
size needed.*

Cattail Lamp
235%

4 round
balls

Lamp Base
235%

Five Drawer Chest
120%

Flys

String

Hooks

Bobbles

Worms

Patterns

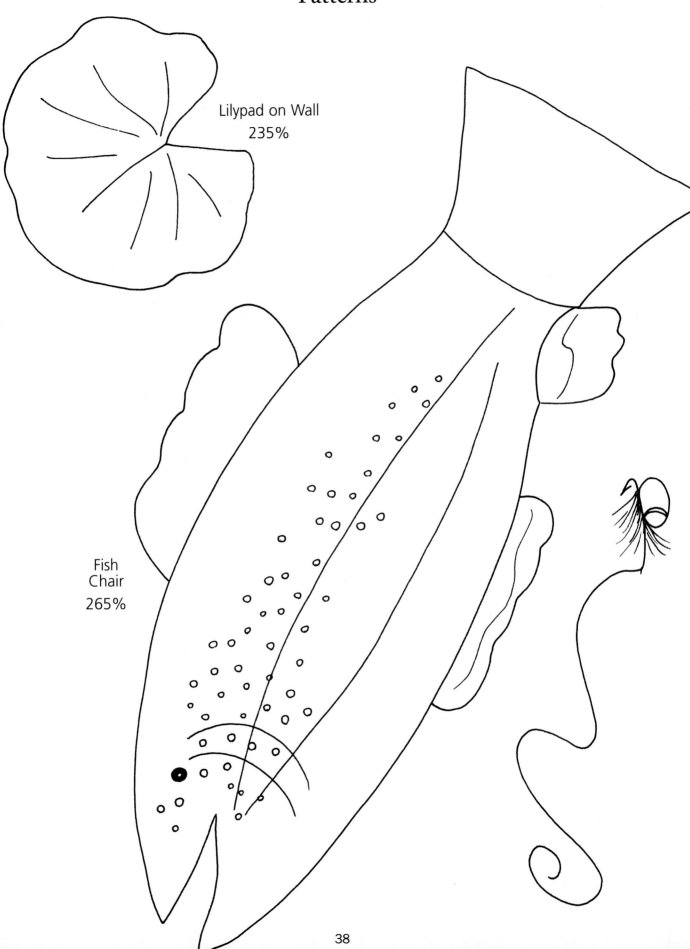

Lilypad on Wall
235%

Fish
Chair
265%

Patterns

Alligator
Wall
Design
600%

Wood Cutout (on Floorcloth)
125%

*Enlarge Patterns at % given or
to size needed.*

GATHER THESE SUPPLIES

FolkArt® Acrylic Colors:
Amethyst 654 (Metallic)
Blue Sapphire 656 (Metallic)
Butter Pecan 939
Emerald Green 653 (Metallic)
Engine Red 436
Green Forest 448
Inca Gold 676 (Metallic)
Licorice 938
Rose Shimmer 652 (Metallic)
Sunflower 432
Thicket 924
Wicker White 901

FolkArt® Artists' Pigment™ Colors:
Dioxazine Purple 463
Yellow Ochre 917

FolkArt® One Stroke™ Brushes:
Flats – sizes #12, 3/4", 1", #6 and 1-1/2"
Scruffy brush
Script #2

Painting Surface:
• Pre-painted Walls (Use satin or eggshell latex wall paint as a base for your decorative painting. This wall started off-white.)
• Wood crown-shaped mirror frame
• Vinyl flooring for floorcloth (You will use the backside of vinyl flooring to paint floorcloth. Canvas can also be used to make floorcloth.)

Other Supplies:
FolkArt® One Stroke™ Sponge Painters 1195
FolkArt® Floating Medium 868
FolkArt® ClearCote™ Matte Acrylic Sealer 789
Flat bottom jewels
Jewel glue
Wood glue
Household Sponge
Painter's Tape

Painted Wall Designs

PREPARATION

1. Transfer or draw outline of castle on the wall.
2. If your wall is not white, use a moistened sponge to fill in the castle with Wicker White.

PAINT THE DESIGN

Castle:

1. Load a 3/4" flat brush with Wicker White and sideload one edge of the brush with Licorice, then work in Floating Medium. Outline the castle walls keeping the Licorice side of the brush on the outside.
2. ROOF/TOWERS: Double load the #12 flat brush with Wicker White and Licorice, then work in Floating Medium. Start at the bottom of the tower roof line to paint the rows of shingles. Each row going up should have fewer shingles than the row below it. The tops of the outside shingles on each end of a row should angle slightly inward toward the tip of the tower. The shingles in between are painted straight up. Starting on the chisel edge, with the Licorice side down, make the shingle by pushing the bristle down, slide over and back to the chisel edge forming a "U." The last shingle at the top is made in a teardrop shape by starting on the chisel edge, pushing the bristles out, and sliding back to the chisel edge.
3. PITCHED ROOF: Double load the #12 flat brush with Wicker White and Licorice, then work in Floating Medium. Start on chisel edge, push down, wiggle, pull and stand up on the chisel. Start shingles on the lower edge of the roof line and make a complete row. On the rows above, stagger the shingles.
4. WINDOWS AND DETAILS: Double load the #12 flat brush with Wicker White and Licorice, then work in Floating Medium to outline the windows and other details.
5. PENNANT FLAGS: Load the #12 flat brush with Floating Medium and sideload metallic Emerald Green. Paint a flag. Repeat with Rose Shimmer, then paint two more flags with metallic Amethyst in the same manner. Load the script liner with Inca Gold and paint the flagpoles.
6. JEWELS: Glue jewels on the tower and at the base of flagpole.

Hills:

Load a moistened sponge with Thicket and Butter Pecan. With the Thicket side up, draw in hills, adding more Butter Pecan at bottom of the hills. Pick up more Thicket and add another layer of hills. Continue filling in the foreground.

Diamond Border:

1. Cut a diamond shaped stencil 12-1/2" by 8".
2. Use a sponge painter to fill in stencil. Alternate colors using metallic Rose Shimmer, metallic Emerald Green, metallic Amethyst, and Inca Gold.
3. Glue jewels where points meet.

Boxes With Jester:

1. BOX TO THE SIDE: Moisten sponge painter and pick up metallic Amethyst. With the straight edge of the sponge outline and fill in box. Load sponge painter with Dioxazine Purple and paint triangles on the box.

2. BOTTOM OF STACKED BOXES: Load a moistened sponge painter with Green Forest and paint the large area on the bottom box. Load the 1" flat brush with Rose Shimmer and fill in triangle areas. Load the 3/4" flat brush with Inca Gold. Add Floating Medium and paint stripes on the rose triangles. Then paint circles at the ends of the triangles.

3. TOP OF STACKED BOXES: Load a moistened sponge painter with Wicker White and paint box. Sideload a little Licorice on one edge and shade side and half circle. Load the 1" flat brush with Licorice and paint half circle. When dry, add triangle of Inca Gold.

Jester on Boxes:

1. Load moistened sponge painter with Wicker White and paint face, neck, hand, and socks.

2. Add Licorice to one corner of sponge painter and, with your finger on that corner, outline those areas to add shading.

3. Load moistened sponge painter with Amethyst. Paint clothes and cap. Sideload sponge with Dioxazine Purple. Keeping your finger on the Dioxazine corner, add shading to the jester's clothes and the cap.

4. Double load the 1" flat brush with Emerald Green and Green Forest. Keeping Green Forest to outer edge, paint collar, sleeves, and top of cap.

5. Load the 1" flat brush with Licorice and paint shoes.

6. Double load the #12 flat brush with Sunflower and Inca Gold. Paint mask on face and balls on tassels of the cap and on the shoes.

7. Dip handle end of brush into Inca gold. Paint dots on face.

8. Load the #12 flat brush with Inca gold and paint lace around sleeves. On the chisel edge of #12 flat, paint gold stripes on the jester's clothing.

9. Load the # 6 flat brush with Engine Red and paint lips, starting at the outside and pushing and pulling in to the chisel edge.

10. Paint the eye as shown on "Angelfish & Eyes" Painting Worksheet.

Continued on page 44

11. Load the #2 script liner with inky Licorice and add details to the face.

12. Load moistened sponge painter with Yellow Ochre, outline, and fill in large mask and stick handle.

13. Double load the 3/4" flat brush with Yellow Ochre and Floating Medium and paint details on mask face and stick. With same loaded brush, sideload Licorice and paint eyes on mask. Load the #2 script liner into inky Licorice and outline mask eyes and mask hole details.

14. Load the #12 flat brush with Amethyst and paint ribbons on mask.

Jester on Bubbles:

1. Load moistened sponge painter with Floating Medium and sideload into metallic Blue Sapphire. Outline bubbles with blue edge, and fill in by rubbing in circles.

2. Load moistened sponge painter with Wicker White and paint jester's face, neck, hand, and socks. Add Licorice to one corner of sponge painter and, with your finger on that corner, outline those areas to add shading.

3. Load moistened sponge painter with metallic Rose Shimmer. Outline and fill in the rose portion of jester's clothing. Pick up a little Wicker White on one corner to add highlights. Paint the green portion of the clothing with metallic Emerald Green mixed with Green Forest. Apply this with a sponge painter.

4. Load the #6 flat brush with Engine Red and paint lips, starting at the outside, pushing and pulling in to the chisel edge.

5. Load the #2 script liner with inky Licorice and paint bubble-blowing wand and face details. Refer to "Angelfish & Eyes" Painting Worksheet.

6. Load the #12 flat brush with Inca Gold and paint the stripes on his cap. Use the #2 script liner with inky Inca Gold to add detail and stripes to clothing.

7. Load the #12 flat brush with Yellow Ochre and paint ball on the shoe.

8. Glue jewels at the ends of tassels on jester's cap. ◻

Jester Floorcloth

PREPARATION

1. Cut out vinyl floorcloth according to pattern and basecoat the backside with Wicker White. Let dry.
2. Load a moistened sponge painter with Inca Gold and pounce entire floorcloth. Let dry.
3. Transfer design.

PAINT THE DESIGN

Jesters:

1. Load the 3/4" flat brush with Wicker White and paint the faces.
2. Sideload the same loaded brush with Licorice and shade faces and eyes.
3. Load the #12 flat brush with Wicker White and paint ribbons.
4. Double load the #12 flat brush with Floating Medium and Rose Shimmer.

Paint masks around the eyes by pushing hard on the chisel edge of the bush and lifting to the chisel at the end of the stroke. Then paint the mouths, keeping the rose on outer edge of the lips.

5. Use the 1" flat brush to paint the caps. One is Rose Shimmer and the other is metallic Emerald Green. Load the 3/4" flat brush with Inca Gold and paint stripes on the rose cap. On the chisel edge of the 3/4" flat brush, paint Inca Gold stripes on the green cap.
6. Load the #12 flat brush with Inca Gold and paint balls on the ends of the green cap. Load the #12 flat brush with metallic Amethyst and paint balls on the ends of the rose cap.

Diamond Border:

1. Use the stencil (from wall border) or use painter's tape to mask off the diamonds on the edge. The corners are elongated and they stay Inca Gold.
2. Load a moistened sponge painter with Rose Shimmer and pounce every third diamond.
3. Load moistened sponge painter with metallic Emerald Green and pounce the diamonds to the left of the rose diamonds.
4. Load moistened sponge painter with metallic Amethyst and pounce the diamonds to the left of the green diamonds.

Finish:

When dry, spray the floorcloth with matte acrylic sealer. ❑

Jester with Bubbles
600%

Crown Mirror

PREPARATION

1. Basecoat mirror frame and balls with Wicker White. Let dry.
2. Load the 1-1/2" flat brush with Inca Gold and re-basecoat frame.

PAINT THE DESIGN

1. Paint two balls with metallic Rose Shimmer, two balls with metallic Emerald Green, and one ball with metallic Amethyst.
2. Load the #2 script liner with inky Licorice and add loose detail lines.
3. Glue balls to top of mirror. ❑

Patterns

Jester Floorcloth
270%

Floorcloth Outline:
See diamond pattern
on page 49.

*Enlarge Patterns at % given or
to size needed.*

Patterns

Crown Mirror
350%

Jester on Box
600%

Enlarge Patterns at % given or to size needed.

Patterns

Diamond Pattern
200%

For Wall: Repeat diamond along wall on center line.

For Floorcloth: Align 6 diamonds side by side along straight line for width, 5 diamonds for height. Draw points at corners. Use photo as guide.

Castle
465%

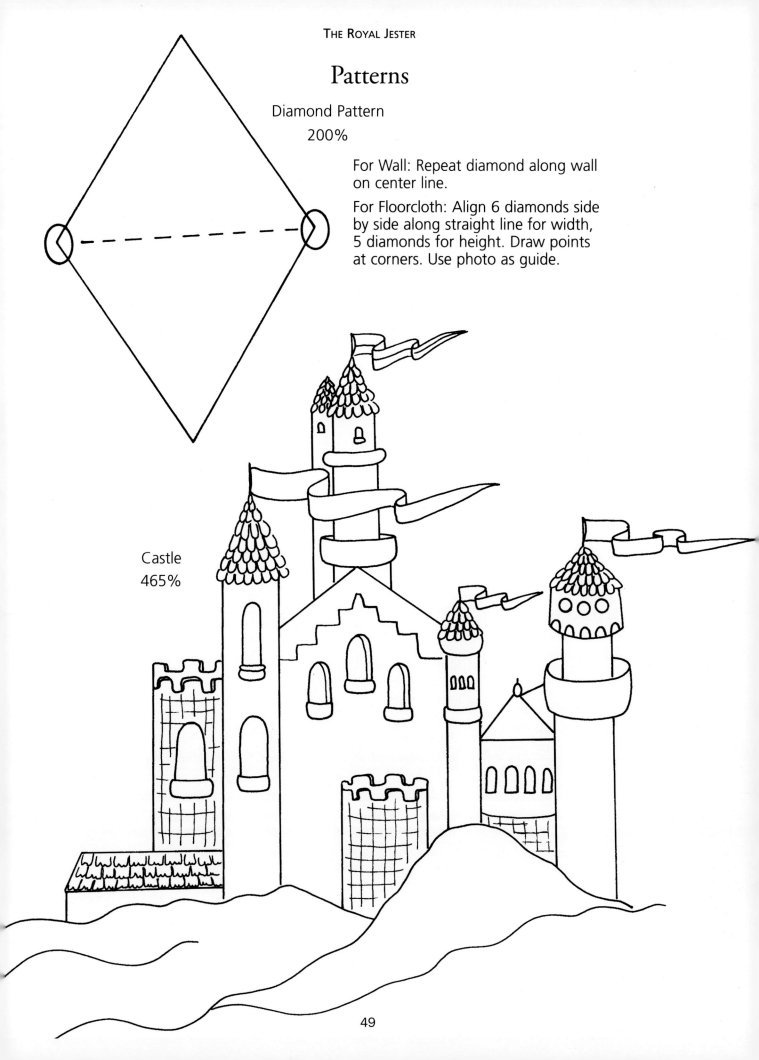

THE GARDEN SWING

GATHER THESE SUPPLIES

FolkArt® Acrylic Colors:

Berry Wine 434
Butter Pecan 939
Dark Plum 469
Italian Sage 467
Licorice 938
Maple Syrup 945
Midnight 964
Raspberry Sherbert 966
Rose Garden 754
School Bus Yellow 736
Sterling Blue 441
Sunflower 432
Thicket 924
Wicker White 901

FolkArt® Artists' Pigment™ Colors:

Burnt Umber 462
Dioxazine Purple 463
Yellow Ochre 917

FolkArt® One Stroke™ Brushes:

Flats – sizes #6, #8, #12, 3/4" and 1"
Script liner – size #2
Scruffy brushes – sizes regular
and small

Painting Surfaces:

• Pre-painted Walls (Use eggshell or satin finish latex paint. These walls were painted a very pale blue.)
• Vinyl flooring remnant, 36" x 48" for floorcloth (You will be painting on the backside of the vinyl flooring. Canvas can also be used for the floorcloth.)
• Battenburg bedspread
• Battenburg throw pillow
• Wood birdhouse clothes pole*
• Wood birdhouse bench*
• Five wood birdhouse plaques* (shown hanging from tree and attached to wall)
* www.jmoriginalcreations.com

Other Supplies:

FolkArt® One Stroke™ Sponge
Painters 1195
FolkArt® Floating Medium 868
FolkArt® Textile Medium 794
(for bedding projects)
FolkArt® ClearCote™ Matte Acrylic
Sealer 789
Foam plates – a 6" and a 10"

Painted Walls & Birdhouse Plaques

PREPARATION

1. Basecoat plaques with Wicker White. Let dry.
2. Transfer designs to walls and plaques. (This can be done as you need them.) Paint the plaques as variations of all the other birdhouses in this room. They can be painted like the birdhouses in back of bed or painted like bench or floorcloth. No specific instructions are given for the plaque designs.

PAINT THE DESIGN

Tree:

1. With a pencil, lightly sketch the size of the tree you want and the branches.
2. Using a dampened sponge painter, dip straight side of sponge into Butter Pecan and then sideload into Maple Syrup. With Maple Syrup to outer edge, paint outline of trunk. Now pulling from that edge into a circular motion, work paint toward center of tree to fill in trunk. You might need to pick up a touch of Floating Medium for smoother strokes.
3. Occasionally sideload a touch of Maple Syrup on edge of sponge to add depth, details and knots.
4. BRANCHES: Load the 1" flat brush with Butter Pecan and sideload Maple Syrup. With Maple Syrup to outer edge, paint branches. You might need to pick up a touch of Floating Medium to have smoother looking strokes. Refer to "Branch/Vines, Seaweed, Waterlily & Frog" Painting Worksheet, using colors given here.
5. VINES: Double load the 1" brush with Thicket and Sunflower. On chisel edge, leading with Sunflower, paint vines to wrap around tree trunk. Refer to "Branch/Vines, Seaweed, Waterlily & Frog" Painting Worksheet, using colors given here.
6. LARGER LEAVES: With same brush and Thicket turned to outer edge, paint heart shaped wiggle leaves. Starting on chisel edge, lean bristles down and while pivoting on Sunflower, move bristles back and forth to form a shell-like shape. Then keep turning the green toward you as you slide brush back to a chisel edge. Make sure brush is on chisel edge before finishing stroke, this will give you a nice tip on your leaf. Repeat on opposite side to complete leaf. Some of these leaves have one wiggle side and the other side smooth. For the smooth side, lean bristles, push, and slide brush to meet tip of opposite side. On chisel edge, leading with Sunflower, paint stem immediately after painting each leaf. Refer to "Leaves & Cattail" Painting Worksheet, using colors given here.

Continued on page 52

Wall & Birdhouse Plaques (cont.)

7. SMALL ONE STROKE LEAVES: Double load the #12 flat brush with Thicket and Sunflower. With Thicket to outer edge, push bristles down while pivoting on Sunflower, turn green side at a 45- degree angle and, while pulling, lift to chisel edge to get a nice tip on leaf. Refer to "Leaves & Cattail" Painting Worksheet, using colors given here.

8. Double load the scruffy brush with Thicket and Sunflower. You load the scruffy brush by pouncing one half of brush into Sunflower and other half into Thicket. Holding the scruffy brush in a vertical position, pounce moss at bottom of tree.

Swing:

1. Pencil in seat of swing or transfer a pattern to the wall for swing seat. Now place the 10" foam plate on center of swing and draw a circle. This is the brim of the hat. Draw a smaller circle using 6" foam plate inside the first circle for crown of hat.

2. Rub a dampened sponge painter into Butter Pecan. Basecoat swing.

3. Load the #12 flat brush with Floating Medium and sideload into Maple Syrup. With Maple Syrup to outer edge, paint shading and accents on swing, giving it a wood look.

Hat:

1. Rub the round side of dampened sponge painter into Butter Pecan and a touch of Wicker White. Basecoat hat, making sure that you shade darker areas with Butter Pecan. Allow to dry.

2. Double load the 3/4" flat brush with Butter Pecan and Floating Medium. On chisel edge, leading with Floating Medium, paint criss-cross lines (crosshatching) on top of hat.

3. BOW AND RIBBON: Double load the #12 flat brush with Sterling Blue and Wicker White. With Sterling Blue to outer edge and brush on its flat edge, paint ribbon around hat. To paint bow, start on chisel edge, slide down and press bristles as you come around, and slide back up on chisel to create loops. To paint trailing ribbon, start on chisel, press, pull, and turn as you move brush. Refer to "Critters" Painting Worksheet, using colors given here.

Wild Rose and Buds on Hat:

Refer to "Flower" Painting Worksheet #2, using colors given here.

1. Double load the 3/4" brush with Berry Wine and Wicker White. With Wicker White to outer edge, paint five or six shell-like petals to form outer skirt of rose. Paint these petals by pushing on bristles and, while pivoting on Berry Wine side, move brush back and forth until you create a shell-like petal. Overlap petals. Repeat and paint second row and third row of petals, if necessary.

2. With the same loaded brush, paint two to three shell strokes together to form buds.

3. Load the small scruffy with Thicket and Sunflower. Pounce center of rose.

4. Using the #12 flat brush double loaded with Thicket and Sunflower, paint one stroke leaves and smaller leaves around the hat brim.

5. Paint two or three rose buds along brim using #12 brush double loaded with Berry wine and Wicker White. Paint buds by making two or three overlapping shell-like petals.

6. Add little clusters of wisteria along brim using the scruffy brush loaded with Dark Plum and Wicker White.

Wisteria & Vine From Tree Branch to Swing:

1. Double load the 1" flat brush with Thicket and Sunflower. On chisel edge, leading with Sunflower, paint branches intertwining to form a vine. Make sure to paint some coming from underneath the swing seat. Refer to photo of project.

2. Double load the 3/4" flat brush with Thicket and Sunflower. Paint one stroke leaves along the vine as previously instructed.

3. Double load the #12 flat brush with Thicket and Sunflower. Paint smaller One Stroke leaves in clusters of two or three along the vine.

4. WISTERIA: Double load the scruffy brush with Dark Plum and Wicker White by pouncing one half of brush into Wicker White and other half into Dark Plum. Holding the scruffy brush in a vertical position, with Dark Plum to outer edge, pounce brush straight up and down in a circular motion, then lean brush to side in order to paint tapered tail of flower. *Refer to "Feather, Moss & Wisteria" Painting Worksheet, using colors given here.*

Flower Basket:

Refer to "Feather, Moss & Wisteria" Painting Worksheet, using colors given below.

1. Transfer pattern to wall.

2. Load the 1" flat brush with Butter Pecan and pick up a touch of Floating Medium for smoother strokes. On chisel edge, using downward strokes, paint vertical lines.

3. Load the 1" flat brush with Butter Pecan. On the chisel edge, paint horizontal strokes by pushing and pulling to form weaving pattern on basket. Make sure to over lap rows in order to have the weave effect.

4. Load the #12 flat brush with Butter Pecan. Using "C" strokes, paint handle of basket.

Moss, Flowers & Leaves in Basket:

1. MOSS: Double load the scruffy brush with Thicket and Butter Pecan. and pick up a touch of Sunflower on the Butter Pecan side. (Load by pouncing one half of brush straight up and down into the side puddle of one color; repeat for other side with second color.) Pounce moss by holding brush straight up and down with Thicket to outer edge. Make sure your entire arm moves in a circular motion and lean brush to its side to give tapered effect. *Refer to*

Continued on page 54

Wall & Birdhouse Plaques (cont.)
"Feather, Moss & Wisteria" Painting Worksheet, using colors given here.

2. IRIS: Double load the 1" brush with Dark plum and Wicker White with a little Dioxazine Purple on the plum side. Turn plum side to outer edge on most petals but turn Wicker White to outer edge on some petals. With Wicker White to outer edge, paint center petal of each flower by pushing, wiggling, and sliding to tip, then lean down and wiggle down to finish stroke. Paint side strokes and add a couple of center strokes.

3. OTHER COLOR COMBINATIONS FOR FLOWERS:
Berry Wine and Wicker White and occasionally pick up a touch of Sunflower on the Wicker White side. Berry Wine and Sunflower with Berry Wine to outer edge.

4. CALYXES AND STEMS: Double load the 1" flat brush with Thicket and Sunflower. On chisel edge and leading with Sunflower, touch base of flower and pull three to four strokes to form calyx of each flower. Pull stems.

5. LEAVES: With Thicket to outer edge and starting on chisel, push, pull, and turn to paint leaves. *Refer to "Leaves & Cattails" Painting Worksheet, using colors given here.*

6. TENDRILS: Load the #2 script liner with inky Thicket. With brush in a vertical position, staying on tip of bristles, paint curliques. Turn two to three circles in one direction, then reverse and paint one or two circles in the opposite direction.

NOTE: There are two variations of birdhouses on the walls. Hanging birdhouses are plaques that have been painted and attached to the wall. The birdhouses on poles above the bed are painted directly on the wall. Instructions are given for the birdhouses above the bed. Paint the plaques using these same colors and instructions, or vary as desired. Before beginning, basecoat the plaques with Wicker White and let dry. The instructions that follow are for birdhouses above the bed moving from left to right.

Birdhouse with Moss Roof:
1. Transfer birdhouse to wall.
2. Dip a dampened sponge painter into Butter Pecan. With the straight edge of the sponge, paint outline of birdhouse, then pull paint in a circular motion toward the center to fill in.
3. Double load the 1" flat brush with Floating Medium and Butter Pecan. With the color side of the brush toward the outer edge, paint shading.
4. DOOR HOLE: Load the 1" flat brush with Butter Pecan and sideload into Maple Syrup. With Maple Syrup to outer edge, paint the hole. Load the #2 script liner with Wicker White and add highlights to hole.
5. POLE: Double load the 3/4" flat brush with Butter Pecan and Wicker White. Add Floating Medium to smooth out your stroke. Paint pole, starting from the birdhouse, by leaning bristles and pulling toward the floor.
6. MOSSY ROOF: Double load scruffy brush with Thicket and Butter Pecan by pouncing one half of brush straight up and down into the side puddle of one color and repeating for other side with second color. Pounce moss on roof, holding brush straight up and down with Thicket to outer edge. Make sure your entire arm moves in a circular motion and lean brush to its side to taper the moss. *Refer to "Feather, Moss & Wisteria" Painting Worksheet, using colors given here.*
7. VINES: Double load the 1" flat brush with Thicket and Butter Pecan. On chisel edge and leading with Butter Pecan, paint vines to wrap around pole.
8. ONE STROKE LEAVES: Double load the 1" flat brush with Thicket and Butter Pecan. With Thicket to outer edge, push bristles down while pivoting on Butter Pecan side, turn green side at a 45-degree angle and, while pulling, lift to chisel edge to get a nice tip on leaf. *Refer to "Leaves & Cattail" Painting Worksheet, using colors given here.* Pull stems into the leaves from the vine while the leaves are wet. Paint leaves along vine on pole and also

roof. paint leaf-clusters on mossy roof. paint leaf-clusters on mossy
9. TENDRILS: Load the #2 script liner with inky Thicket. Keeping brush on a vertical position, paint curliques, making two to three circles in one direction, then paint one to two circles in the other direction. Move your entire arm, not just your wrist. Paint tendrils along vine on pole and paint some among the leaves on roof.
10. BOW AND RIBBON: Double load the #12 flat brush with Sterling Blue and Wicker White and paint bow on the pole at the bottom of the birdhouse. Start on chisel edge and slide down and press bristles as you come around, then slide back up on chisel to create loops. To paint the trailing ribbon, start on chisel edge, press, pull, and turn as you move brush. *Refer to "Critters" Painting Worksheet, using colors given here.*

Yellow Birdhouse with Scallop Roof:
1. Transfer hanging birdhouse to wall.
2. Dip a dampened sponge painter into Yellow Ochre. With the straight edge of the sponge, paint outline of birdhouse then pull paint in a circular motion toward the center to fill in.
3. Double load the 1" flat brush with Floating Medium and Yellow Ochre. With the color side of the brush toward the outer edge, paint shading.
4. DOOR HOLE & PERCH: Load the 1" flat brush with Butter Pecan and sideload into Maple Syrup. With Maple Syrup to outer edge, paint hole. Load the #12 flat brush with Maple Syrup and paint perch on the chisel edge of the brush. Load the #2 script liner with Wicker White and add highlights to hole and perch.
5. POLE: Load the 3/4" flat brush with Butter Pecan and Wicker White. Add Floating Medium to smooth out your stroke. Paint the pole, starting from the birdhouse, by leaning bristles and pulling toward the floor.

6. ROOF: Double load the 3/4" flat brush with Butter Pecan and Burnt Umber. With the Burnt Umber on the lower edge, paint each scallop as follows: Starting on chisel edge, push the bristles out, slide over, and lift back to chisel edge. The tops of the end scallops on each row should be angled toward the tip of the roof. The rows should overlap and each row working upward will have fewer scallops.

7. ROSEBUDS AND LEAVES: *Refer to "Flowers" Painting Worksheet #1, using colors given here.* Load the #12 flat brush with Berry Wine and Wicker White. Start on the chisel edge with the Wicker White upward. Touch brush to surface to make two parallel lines. Keeping the handle of the brush straight up, stand it on chisel edge from one line, push the bristles down, and slide the white side up the hill over to the other line coming back to the chisel. Pick up fresh paint and go back to where you started at the first line on the chisel edge with the white up. Slightly lean the bristles back, then lay the brush down and paint a "U" by going down, over, and back up on the chisel at the second line. The white edges should meet and form a circle. Pick up fresh paint and paint a second "U" slightly below the previous stroke.

8. LEAVES: Double load the #12 flat brush with Thicket and Butter Pecan. Paint One Stroke leaves around the rosebuds and hole. With Thicket to outer edge, push bristles down while pivoting on Butter Pecan, turn the green to a 45-degree angle and, while pulling, lift to chisel edge to get a nice tip on leaf. *Refer to "Leaves & Cattail" Painting Worksheet, using colors given here.* Pull stems into the leaves from the vine while the leaves are wet.

9. TENDRILS: Load the #2 script liner with inky Thicket. Keeping brush on a vertical position, paint curliques, painting two to three circles in one direction, then one or two circles in the other direction. Move your entire arm, not just your wrist.

10. MOSS: Double load the scruffy brush with Thicket and Butter Pecan. Pounce moss along one side of roof. *Refer to "Feather, Moss & Wisteria" Painting Worksheet, using colors given here.*

Rose Birdhouse with Thatched Roof:

1. Transfer birdhouse to wall.

2. Dip a dampened sponge painter into Butter Pecan. With the straight edge of the sponge, paint outline of birdhouse, then pull paint in a circular motion toward the center to fill in.

3. Double load the 1" flat brush with Floating Medium and Rose Garden. With the color side of the brush toward the outer edge, paint shading.

4. DOOR HOLE: Load the 1" flat brush with Butter Pecan and sideload into Maple Syrup. With Maple Syrup to outer edge, paint hole. Load the #2 script liner with Wicker White and add highlights to hole.

5. ROOF: Load the 3/4" flat brush with Burnt Umber and Wicker White. On chisel edge, leading with Wicker White, stroke from the bottom to the top, layering rows to the top.

6. BASE AND POLE: Load the 3/4" flat brush with Burnt Umber and Wicker White. Add Floating Medium to smooth out your stroke. Paint the base on birdhouse. Paint pole, starting from the birdhouse, on the chisel edge; pull toward the floor.

7. PERCH: Load the #12 flat brush with Maple Syrup and paint perch on the chisel edge of the brush. Load the #2 script liner with Wicker White and add highlights to perch.

8. MOSS: Double load the scruffy brush with Thicket and Butter Pecan. Pounce moss along one side of the base. *Refer to "Feather, Moss & Wisteria" Painting Worksheet, using colors given here.*

Brown Birdhouse with Scalloped Roof:

1. Transfer hanging birdhouse to wall.

2. Dip a dampened sponge painter into Butter Pecan. With the straight edge of the sponge, paint outline of bird-house, then pull paint in a circular motion toward the center to fill in.

3. Double load the 1" flat brush with Floating Medium and Butter Pecan. With the color side of the brush toward the outer edge, paint shading.

4. DOOR HOLE: Load the 1" flat brush with Butter Pecan and sideload into Maple Syrup. With Maple Syrup to outer edge, paint hole. Load the #2 script liner with Wicker White and add highlights to hole.

5. POLE: Load the 3/4" flat brush with Butter Pecan and Wicker White. Add Floating Medium to smooth out your stroke. Paint the pole, starting from the birdhouse, by leaning bristles and pulling toward the floor.

6. PERCH: Load the #12 flat brush with Maple Syrup and paint perch on the chisel edge of the brush. Load the #2 script liner with Wicker White and add highlights to perch.

7. BOW: Load the #2 script liner with inky Midnight. Paint string bow on the perch. Keeping brush in a vertical position, paint the bow on the tip of the bristles making each loop individually. Paint each loop down and then up. Add tails to the loop and put in a little "C" stroke for a knot in the middle.

8. ROOF: Double load the 3/4" flat brush with Wicker White and Berry Wine. With the Berry Wine on the lower edge, paint each scallop as follows: Starting on the chisel edge, push the bristles out, slide over, and lift back to chisel edge. The tops of the end scallops on each row should be angled toward the tip of the roof. The rows should overlap, and each row working upward will have fewer scallops.

9. MOSS: Double load the scruffy brush with Thicket and Butter Pecan. Pounce moss up and around pole, keeping the Thicket side of the brush up. Move your entire arm and do not turn the brush. Lean brush to trail off on one side of birdhouse. *Refer to*

Continued on next page

Wall & Birdhouse Plaques (cont.)

"Feather, Moss & Wisteria" Painting Worksheet, using colors given here.

Plum Birdhouse with Tin Roof:

1. Dip a dampened sponge painter into Dark Plum. With the straight edge of the sponge, paint outline of birdhouse, then pull paint in a circular motion toward the center to fill in.

2. Double load the 1" flat brush with Floating Medium and Dark Plum. With the color side of the brush toward the outer edge, paint shading.

3. DOOR HOLES: Load the 1" flat brush with Butter Pecan and sideload into Maple Syrup. With Maple Syrup to outer edge, paint holes. Load the #2 script liner with Wicker White and add highlights to holes.

4. BASE & POLE: Load the 3/4" flat brush with Burnt Umber and Wicker White. Paint base of birdhouse using slight "C" strokes. Paint pole, starting from the birdhouse, by leaning bristle and pulling toward the floor. Add Floating Medium to smooth out your stroke.

5. ROOF: Double load the 1" flat brush with Butter Pecan and Burnt Umber. With the Burnt Umber edge down, start at the top of the birdhouse on the left, lay bristles down, and pull across two-thirds of the birdhouse. Continue stroking up the roof, creating two-thirds of a cone shape. Pick up a little Floating Medium to smooth out the strokes. Now do the same thing from the right side but stand brush up to the chisel to make the appearance of the edge of the tin. Dip the handle end of the brush into Burnt Umber and dot along the line to make nail heads.

6. VINES AND FLOWERS: Double load the 1" flat brush with Thicket and Sunflower. On chisel edge and leading with Sunflower, paint vines to wrap around pole. With Thicket to outer edge, paint heart shape wiggle leaves. Starting on chisel edge, lean bristles down and, while pivoting on Sunflower side, move bristles back and forth to form a shell-like shape; then keep turning green toward you as you slide brush back to a chisel edge. Make sure brush is on chisel edge before finishing stroke. This will give you a nice tip on your leaf. Repeat on opposite side to complete leaf. Some of these leaves have one wiggle side and one smooth side. For the smooth side, lean bristles, push, and slide brush to meet tip of opposite side. On chisel edge, leading with Sunflower, paint stem immediately after painting each leaf. *Refer to "Leaves & Cattail" Painting Worksheet, using colors given here.*

7. LEAVES: For one stroke leaves, with Thicket to outer edge, push bristles down while pivoting on Sunflower side, turn green to a 45-degree angle and, while pulling, lift to chisel edge to get a nice tip on leaf. *Refer to "Leaves & Cattail" Painting Worksheet, using colors given here.*

8. MOSS: Double load the scruffy brush with Thicket and Butter Pecan by pouncing one-half of brush into Thicket and other half into Butter Pecan. Keeping brush in a vertical position, pounce moss over vine at the right corner of the birdhouse bottom.

9. BEGIN FLOWERS AND BUDS: *Refer to "Flower" Painting Worksheet #1, using colors given here.* Double load the 1" flat brush with Berry Wine and Wicker White. With Wicker White to outer edge, paint five or six elongated shell-like petals to form flower. You paint these petals by pushing on bristles and, while pivoting on Berry Wine side, move brush back and forth until you create a shell-like petal. Overlap petals.

10. With the same loaded brush, paint two or three shell strokes together to form buds.

11. Load the small scruffy brush with Thicket and Sunflower. Pounce center of the flowers.

12. Double load the 1" flat brush with Thicket and Sunflower. On chisel edge, leading with Sunflower, touch base of flower and pull three or four strokes to form calyx. Pull stem.

13. TENDRILS: Load the #2 script liner with inky Thicket. Keeping brush on a vertical position, paint curliques, painting two or three circles in one direction, then one or two circles in the other direction. Move your entire arm, not just your wrist.

Bluebirds:

Refer to "Critters" Painting Worksheet, using colors given below.

1. Paint several birds flying around birdhouses, varying their body positions. Load the #12 flat brush with Midnight and Wicker White. Paint top part of bird's bodies.

2. Load the #12 flat brush with Berry Wine and Wicker White. Paint cheeks and lower part of bodies.

3. Load the #12 flat brush with Midnight and Wicker White. Paint wings and tail.

4. Load the #2 script liner with Yellow Ochre and paint beaks.

5. Dip handle end of brush into Licorice and dot eyes.

6. Load the #2 script liner with inky Licorice and paint detail on the beaks.

7. Dip handle end of brush into Wicker White and dot highlights in eyes.

8. Load script liner with inky Berry Wine and add string ribbon bows to the necks of some of the bluebirds. □

*Bedspread instructions
on next page*

Bedspread

PREPARATION

1. Transfer birdhouse patterns to bedspread and bluebird patterns to throw pillow cover.
2. Place plastic-covered cardboard under the area you are painting for a firm surface and to keep paint from seeping through fabric onto something else.
3. Mix all paint colors with Textile Medium, as directed with the product.

PAINT THE DESIGN

Paint birdhouses on bedspread and bluebirds on throw pillow as directed for these items on walls. ❑

Birdhouse Row Floorcloth

PREPARATION

1. Using pattern, cut birdhouse row from vinyl flooring.
2. Basecoat the backside of the floorcloth with Wicker White (or equivalent color wall paint).

PAINT THE DESIGN

Green Birdhouse:

1. Dip a moistened sponge painter in Italian Sage and fill in the end birdhouse.
2. Double load the 1" flat brush with Thicket and Floating Medium. With Thicket to the outer edge, shade birdhouse.
3. ROOF: Load the 1" flat brush with Thicket and paint roof on birdhouse.
4. HOLES & PERCHES: Load the 1" flat brush with Butter Pecan and sideload into Burnt Umber. With Burnt Umber to outer edge, paint holes and perches. Load the #2 script liner with Wicker White paint and add highlights to the bird holes and the ends of the perches.
5. MOSS: Double load the scruffy brush with Wicker White and Thicket. Holding brush in vertical position, pounce moss at the base of the chimney, along the bottom of the house and up the outside (left) edge of the house. *Refer to "Feather, Moss & Wisteria" Painting Worksheet, using colors given here.*
6. VINES: Load the #12 flat brush with Thicket and Wicker White. Pick up Butter Pecan on the Wicker White side. Paint a vine over the moss on lower left corner of house. Refer to photo of project.
7. LEAVES: Add a couple of grape leaves to the vine. To make the grape leaves, touch chisel edge of brush to make a "V" going out and away from the vine. Then with the Thicket on the outer edge of brush, place the brush on one side of the "V." Push the bristles down and wiggle back and forth as you pull to the side. Come up slightly on the chisel and slide back toward the center of the leaf. Push the bristles back down, wiggle, and pivot on the inner edge of the brush causing the brush to turn. Then slide to the chisel to make the tip. Now repeat on the other side of the "V." Be careful not to wiggle on top of the side you have all ready completed. On the chisel edge of the brush, slide a stem from the vine into the leaf. Add one stroke leaves to the vine.
8. TENDRILS: Load the #2 script liner with inky Thicket. Keeping brush on a vertical position, paint curliques, making two or three circles in one direction one or two circles in the other direction. Move your entire arm not just your wrist.
9. BOW: Load the #2 script liner with inky Berry Wine and a little Wicker White. Paint string ribbon bows on the perches.

Round Bottom Birdhouse:

1. Load a moistened sponge painter with Butter Pecan and fill in the round-bottomed birdhouse.
2. Double load the 1" flat brush with Wicker White and Floating Medium. With Wicker White to the outer edge, shade birdhouse.
3. LEAVES: Double load the 1" flat brush with Wicker White and Thicket. On chisel edge of brush, push hard and slide up to the chisel, layering rows of leaves. Alternate leading edge of brush to vary shades of leaves.
4. HOLE & PERCH: Load the 1" flat brush with Butter Pecan and sideload into Burnt Umber. With Burnt Umber to outer edge, paint hole and perch.
5. Load the #2 script liner with Wicker White paint and add highlights to the bird hole and the end of the perch.
6. VINE & LEAVES: Load the #12 flat brush with Thicket and Wicker White. Pick up Butter Pecan on the Wicker White side. Paint an arch of vines and one stroke leaves around the hole of the birdhouse.
7. FLOWERS: Double load the #12 flat brush with Wicker White and Midnight. Paint small five petal flowers on the green arch. Stand brush on the chisel, push bristles out, and slide back to chisel. Paint each petal around in a circle. Make buds by not completing circle or small buds by making push-and-pull petals to a center point. Dip end of brush handle in School Bus Yellow and dot centers.
8. BOW: Load the #2 script liner with inky Midnight and a little Wicker White. Paint a string ribbon bow on the perch.

Blue Birdhouse:

1. Dip a moistened sponge painter in Midnight and Wicker White and fill in the next birdhouse (moving to the right).
2. Load the 1" flat brush with Midnight and paint roof on birdhouse.
3. HOLES & PERCHES: Load the 1" flat brush with Butter Pecan and sideload into Burnt Umber. With Burnt Umber to outer edge, paint holes

and perches. Load the #2 script liner with Wicker White paint and add highlights to the bird holes and the ends of the perches.

4. WREATH: Paint grapevine wreath around top hole with the chisel edge of the 1" flat brush double loaded with Butter Pecan and Burnt Umber.

5. ROSEBUDS: Load the #12 flat brush with Berry Wine and Wicker White. Paint rosebuds around the top half of the grapevine wreath. *Refer to "Flower" Painting Worksheet #1, using colors given here.* To make the rosebuds, start on the chisel edge with Wicker White up. Touch brush to surface to make two parallel lines. Keeping the handle of the brush straight up. Stand brush on chisel edge and, from one line, push the bristle down and slide the white side up the hill, over to the other line, and back to the chisel. Pick up fresh paint and go back where you started at the first line on the chisel edge with the white upward. Slightly lean the bristles back, then lay the brush down and paint a "U" by going down, over, and back up on the chisel at the second line. The white edges should meet and form a circle. Pick up fresh paint and paint a second "U" slightly below the previous stroke.

6. LEAVES: Double load the #12 flat brush with Thicket and Butter Pecan and paint one stroke leaves around the rosebuds and hole. With Thicket to outer edge, push bristles down and, while pivoting on Butter Pecan side; turn green to a 45-degree angle and, while pulling, lift to chisel edge to get a nice tip on leaf. *Refer to "Leaves & Cattail" Painting Worksheet, using colors given here.* Pull stems into the leaves from the vine while the leaves are wet.

7. FILLER FLOWERS: Double load the #12 flat brush with Dark Plum and Wicker White. On the chisel edge, leading with Dark Plum, build filler flowers between roses by touching and pulling.

8. BOW: Double load the #12 flat brush with Berry Wine and Wicker White and paint bow at the bottom of the grapevine wreath. To paint the bow, start on chisel edge. Slide down and press bristles as you come around, then slide back up on chisel to create loops. To paint the trailing ribbon, start on chisel, press, pull, and turn as you move brush. Add a "C" to the middle of the bow to make knot. *Refer to "Critters" Painting Worksheet, using colors given here.*

9. TENDRILS: Load the #2 script liner with inky Thicket. Keeping brush on a vertical position, paint curliques all around the wreath, making two or three circles in one direction one or two circles in the other direction. Move your entire arm not just your wrist.

10. MOSS: Double load the scruffy brush with Wicker White and Thicket. Holding brush in vertical position, pounce moss at the base of the chimney and along the bottom of the house.

Yellow Birdhouse:

1. Load a moistened sponge painter in Sunflower and fill in the end birdhouse on the right.

2. Double load the 3/4" flat brush with Yellow Ochre and Floating Medium. With Yellow Ochre to the outer edge, shade birdhouse.

3. HOLES & PERCHES: Load the 1" flat brush with Butter Pecan and sideload into Burnt Umber. With Burnt Umber to outer edge, paint holes and perches. Load the #2 script liner with Wicker White paint and add highlights to the bird holes and the ends of the perches.

4. MOSS: Double load the scruffy brush with Wicker White and Thicket. Holding brush in vertical position, pounce moss on the roof line and along the bottom of the house.

5. VINES: Load the #12 flat brush with Thicket and Wicker White. Paint vines and one stroke leaves on the moss, trailing down the front. *Refer to "Flower" Painting Worksheet #2, using colors given here.* Load the #12 flat brush with Thicket and Italian Sage. Add a couple of grape leaves to the vine.

6. TENDRILS: Load the #2 script liner with inky Thicket. Keeping brush in a vertical position, paint curliques among the greenery on the roof, making two or three circles in one direction one or two circles in the other direction. Move your entire arm not just your wrist.

7. BOW: Load the #2 script liner with inky Berry Wine and a little Wicker White. Paint string ribbon bows on the middle perch.

8. FINISH: When dry, spray floorcloth with matte acrylic sealer. ❑

Birdhouse Clothes Pole

PREPARATION

1. Basecoat white.
2. Load the 1" flat brush with Dark Plum and water. Color-wash the birdhouse. Color wash the roof with the 1" flat brush loaded with Maple Syrup and water.
3. When dry, transfer any patterns you need.

PAINT THE DESIGN

1. Double load the scruffy brush with Thicket and Wicker White. Pounce moss on different areas of the roof and birdhouse, including wreath around bottom hole of birdhouse.
2. VINES: Double load the 3/4" flat brush with Thicket and Sunflower. On chisel edge and leading with Sunflower, paint vine wrapping around pole. Using same brush with Thicket to outer edge, paint wiggle leaves and one stroke leaves. Double load the #12 flat brush with Thicket and Sunflower. On chisel edge, leading with Sunflower, paint vine around bird holes. With same brush paint one stroke leaves.
3. WISTERIA: Double load the scruffy brush with Wicker White and Dark Plum. Paint wisteria.
4. BOW: Load the #6 flat brush with Wicker White and School Bus Yellow. Paint ribbon bow around perch.
5. TRAILING FLOWERS: With same brush and colors, add trailing flowers.
6. TENDRILS: Load the #2 script liner with inky Thicket. Paint curliques. ❏

Birdhouse Row Bench

PREPARATION

1. Lightly sand bench. Basecoat with two coats of Wicker White (or equivalent color wall paint). Allow to dry.
2. Transfer outlines of birdhouses to bench back. Transfer rose pattern to bench seat.

PAINT THE DESIGN

Color-washing and Shading Birdhouses:

1. Work from left to right. Rub a dampened sponge painter into little water and Butter Pecan. Color-wash the FIRST BIRDHOUSE on the left. Repeat with other birdhouses, using the following color-washes:
SECOND BIRDHOUSE:
Dark Plum
THIRD BIRDHOUSE: Sunflower
FOURTH BIRDHOUSE:
Raspberry Sherbert
2. To add shading, load the 1" flat brush with Floating Medium and sideload with same color as wash for each birdhouse.

Roofs:

1. Load the 1" flat brush with Floating Medium and Maple Syrup. Paint roofs of all birdhouses.
2. CHIMNEYS: Double load #8 flat brush with Butter Pecan and Maple Syrup. With Maple Syrup to outer edge, paint chimneys.

Details:

1. Refer to birdhouse instructions on walls and floorcloth for moss, flowers, and other details.
2. Refer to the iris instructions for flower basket on walls for painting the iris on seat of bench. ❑

Patterns

Enlarge Patterns at % given or to size needed.

Rope
300%

Swing Seat
300%

Hat
300%

Patterns

Wall Plaques
260%

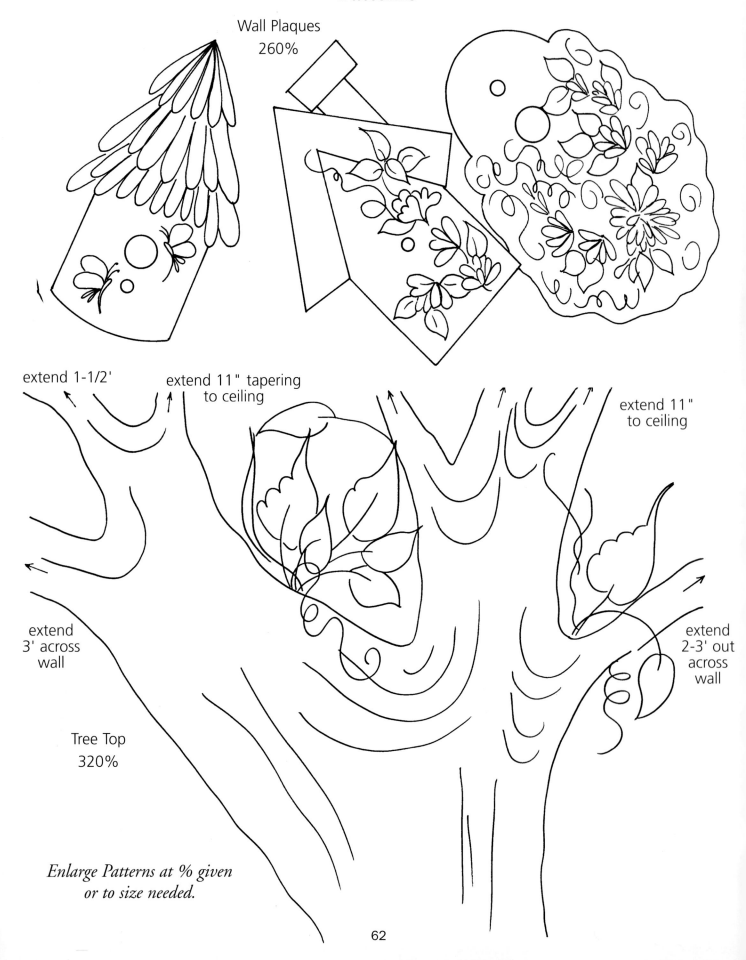

extend 1-1/2'

extend 11" tapering
to ceiling

extend 11"
to ceiling

extend
3' across
wall

extend
2-3' out
across
wall

Tree Top
320%

*Enlarge Patterns at % given
or to size needed.*

Patterns

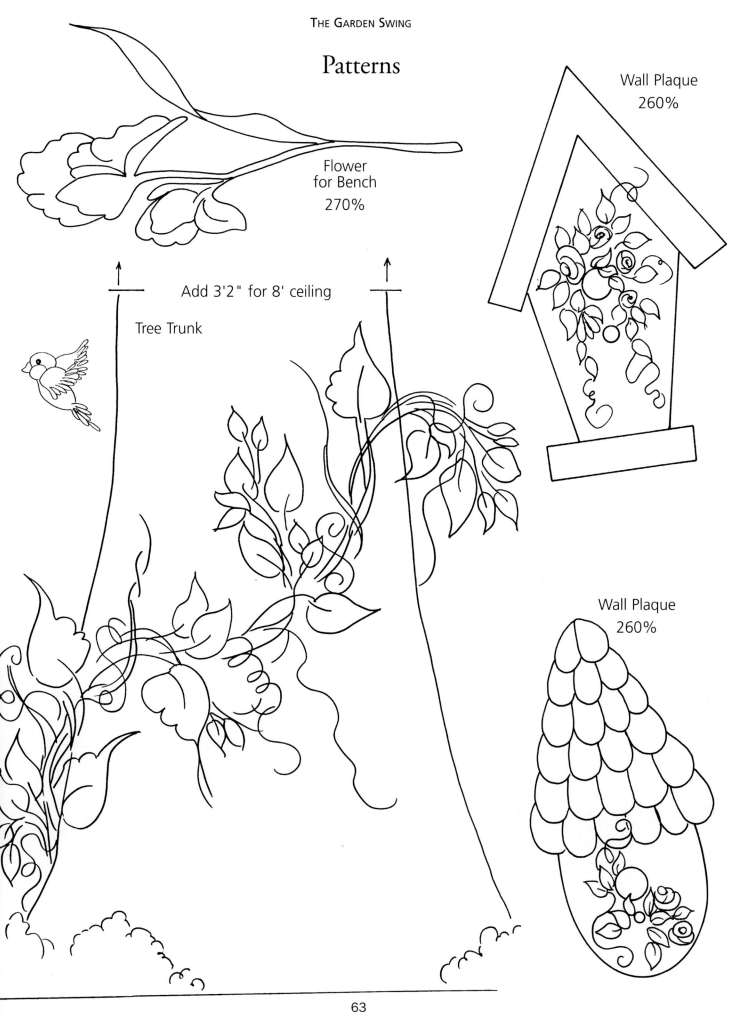

Wall Plaque
260%

Flower
for Bench
270%

Add 3'2" for 8' ceiling

Tree Trunk

Wall Plaque
260%

Patterns

Basket on Wall – 275%
Reverse & repeat for opposite side of basket

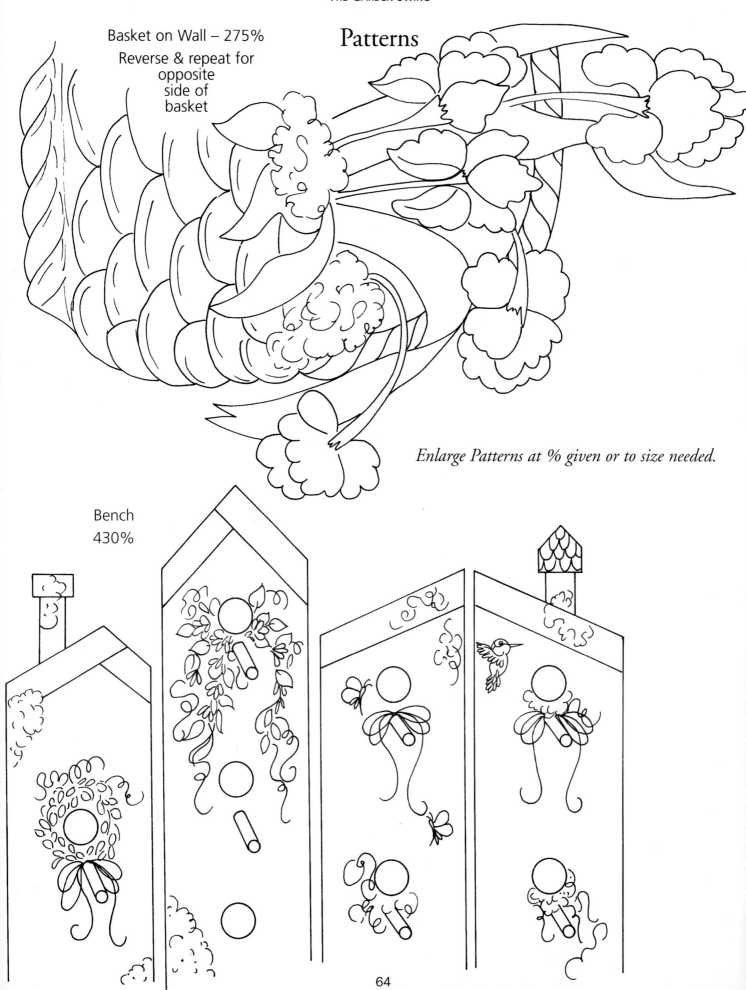

Enlarge Patterns at % given or to size needed.

Bench
430%

Patterns

*Enlarge Patterns at % given or
to size needed.*

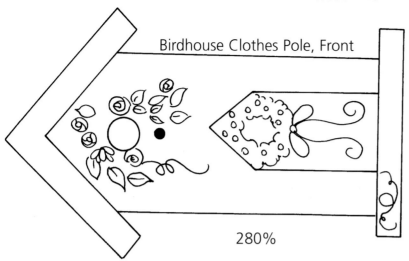

Birdhouse Clothes Pole, Front

280%

Birdhouse Clothes Pole, Roof

Post

Birdhouse Row Floorcloth
465%

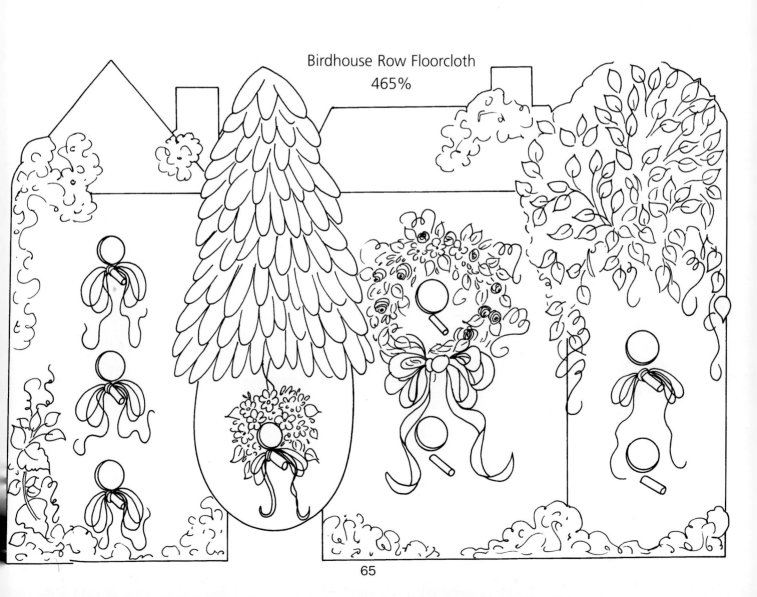

LEAVES & CATTAIL PAINTING WORKSHEET

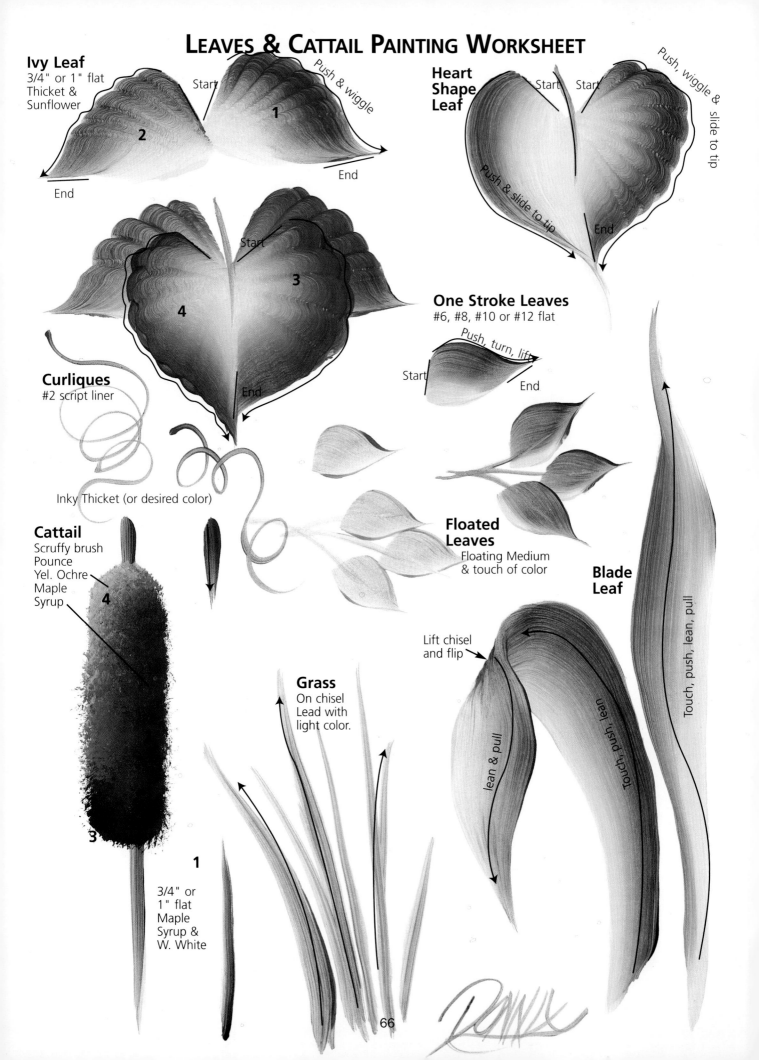

Ivy Leaf
3/4" or 1" flat
Thicket &
Sunflower

Start

Push & wiggle

2

1

End

End

Heart Shape Leaf

Start   Start

Push, wiggle & slide to tip

Push & slide to tip

End

Start

4   3

End

One Stroke Leaves
#6, #8, #10 or #12 flat

Push, turn, lift

Start

End

Curliques
#2 script liner

Inky Thicket (or desired color)

Floated Leaves
Floating Medium
& touch of color

Blade Leaf

Cattail
Scruffy brush
Pounce
Yel. Ochre
Maple
Syrup

4

3

1

3/4" or
1" flat
Maple
Syrup &
W. White

Grass
On chisel
Lead with
light color.

Lift chisel
and flip

lean & pull

Touch, push, lean

Touch, push, lean, pull

FLOWER PAINTING WORKSHEET #1

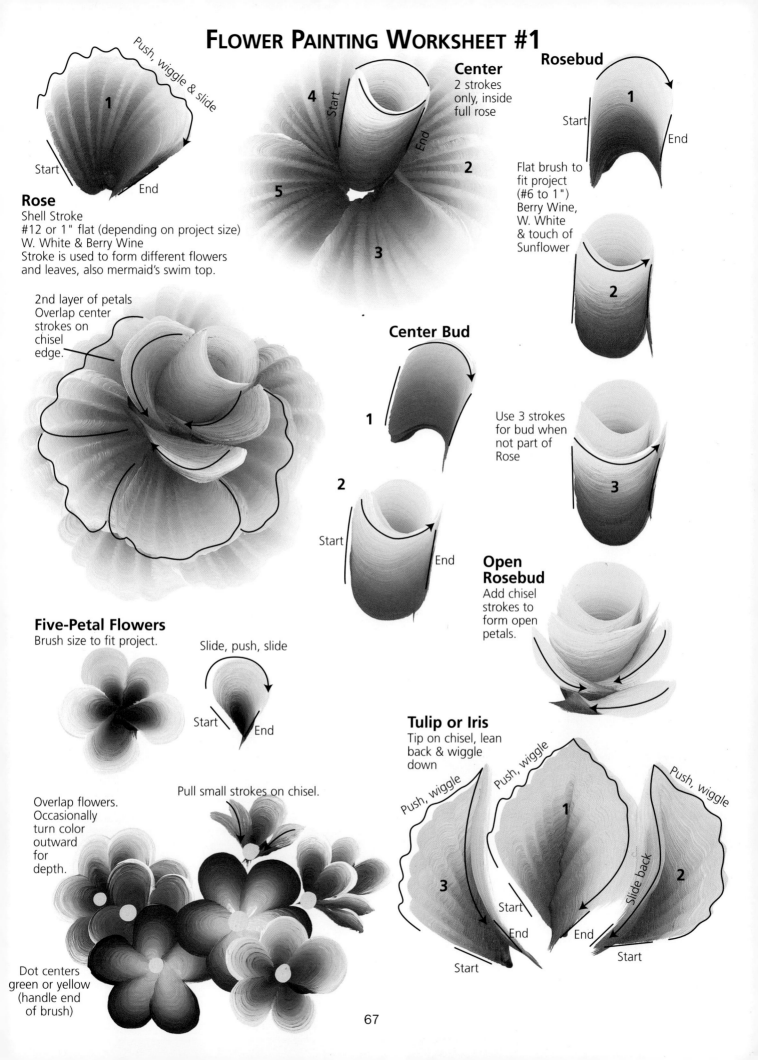

Push, wiggle & slide

1

Start · End

Rose
Shell Stroke
#12 or 1" flat (depending on project size)
W. White & Berry Wine
Stroke is used to form different flowers and leaves, also mermaid's swim top.

4 · Start · **5** · **2** · **3**

Center
2 strokes only, inside full rose

2nd layer of petals
Overlap center strokes on chisel edge.

Rosebud
1
Start · End

Flat brush to fit project (#6 to 1") Berry Wine, W. White & touch of Sunflower

2

Use 3 strokes for bud when not part of Rose

3

Center Bud
1

2
Start · End

Open Rosebud
Add chisel strokes to form open petals.

Five-Petal Flowers
Brush size to fit project.

Slide, push, slide
Start · End

Tulip or Iris
Tip on chisel, lean back & wiggle down

Push, wiggle · Push, wiggle · Push, wiggle · Push, wiggle

1 · **3** · **2**

Start · End · Slide back · End · Start

Start

Overlap flowers. Occasionally turn color outward for depth.

Pull small strokes on chisel.

Dot centers green or yellow (handle end of brush)

67

FLOWER PAINTING WORKSHEET #2

Grass
#12, 3/4"
or 1" flat
Green Forest
& Sch. Bus
Yellow or
Thicket &
Sunflower

On chisel, lead with light color

Wildflower
#12 or 3/4" flat

Touch,
lean,
pull

Work
strokes
left to
right,
over-
lapping
layers.

Daisy
Double
load brush
W. White
& Color

Touch,
lean &
pull
stroke
to
center.

Follow
arrows to
form
flower

Daisy
Center
Lg. or sm.
scruffy brush
Thicket & Sch. Bus Yel.

Pull all
strokes to
center.

Dot center with handle
end of brush

Blossoms
Push, wiggle in & out

#12 or 3/4" flat
Fuchsia & W.
White

1

Start   End

5   2

4   3

Bud &
Trailing Flower

2   1

3 On chisel,
touch &
pull
stroke.

Wild Rose
3/4" or 1" flat

Push, wiggle & slide

1

2

5

3

4

Flower Center
Scruffy
Thicket & Sch. Bus Yel.
Pounce center
#2 script liner
Pull stamens
Dot with Sch. Bus Yel.

Dot with
Thicket &
Sch. Bus Yel.

#2 script
liner

Chrysanthemum

Touch, lean,
pull to center

Layer smaller
strokes.

Overlap
strokes

Pull
strokes
back.

Finer
strokes
on chisel

DONNA

68

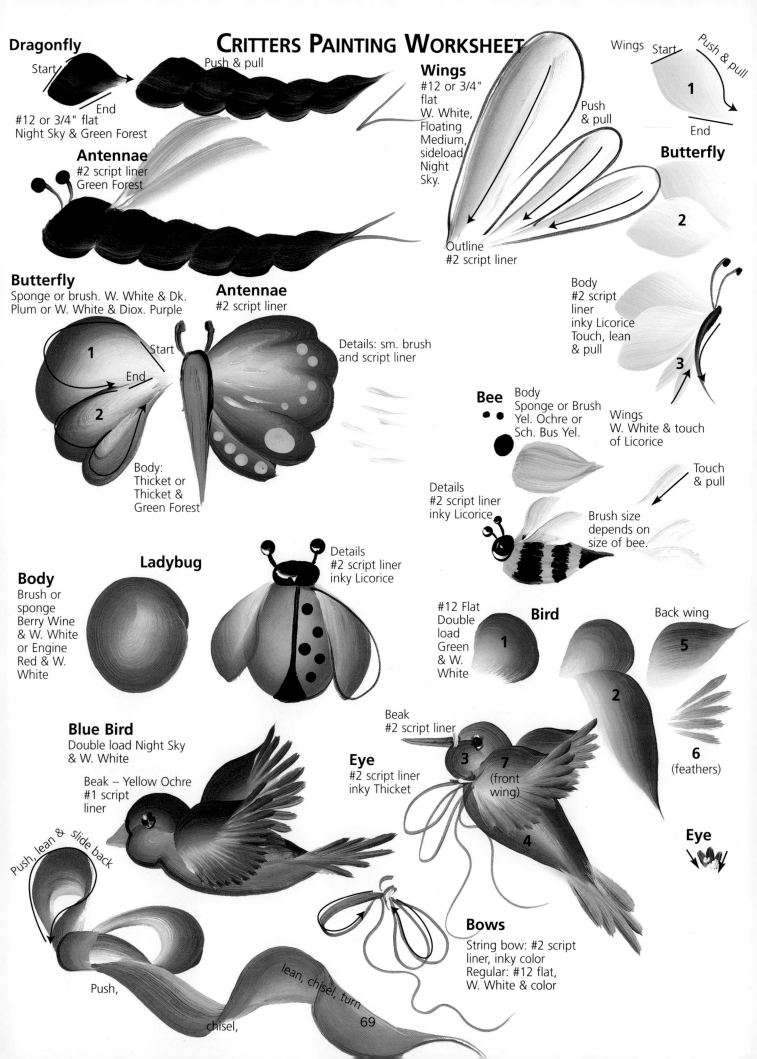

Critters Painting Worksheet

Dragonfly
Start
End
Push & pull
#12 or 3/4" flat
Night Sky & Green Forest

Antennae
#2 script liner
Green Forest

Wings
#12 or 3/4"
flat
W. White,
Floating
Medium,
sideload
Night
Sky.
Push & pull
Outline
#2 script liner

Wings
Start
Push & pull
1
End

Butterfly
2

Butterfly
Sponge or brush. W. White & Dk.
Plum or W. White & Diox. Purple
1
Start
End
2

Antennae
#2 script liner

Details: sm. brush
and script liner

Body:
Thicket or
Thicket &
Green Forest

Body
#2 script
liner
inky Licorice
Touch, lean
& pull
3

Bee Body
Sponge or Brush
Yel. Ochre or
Sch. Bus Yel.

Wings
W. White & touch
of Licorice

Touch
& pull

Details
#2 script liner
inky Licorice

Brush size
depends on
size of bee.

Ladybug

Details
#2 script liner
inky Licorice

Body
Brush or
sponge
Berry Wine
& W. White
or Engine
Red & W.
White

#12 Flat
Double
load
Green
& W.
White
1

Bird

2

Back wing
5

6
(feathers)

Blue Bird
Double load Night Sky
& W. White

Beak – Yellow Ochre
#1 script
liner

Beak
#2 script liner

Eye
#2 script liner
inky Thicket

3
7
(front
wing)
4

Eye

Push, lean & slide back

Bows
String bow: #2 script
liner, inky color
Regular: #12 flat,
W. White & color

Push,
lean, chisel, turn
chisel,
69

BRANCH/VINES, SEAWEED, WATERLILY & FROG PAINTING WORKSHEET

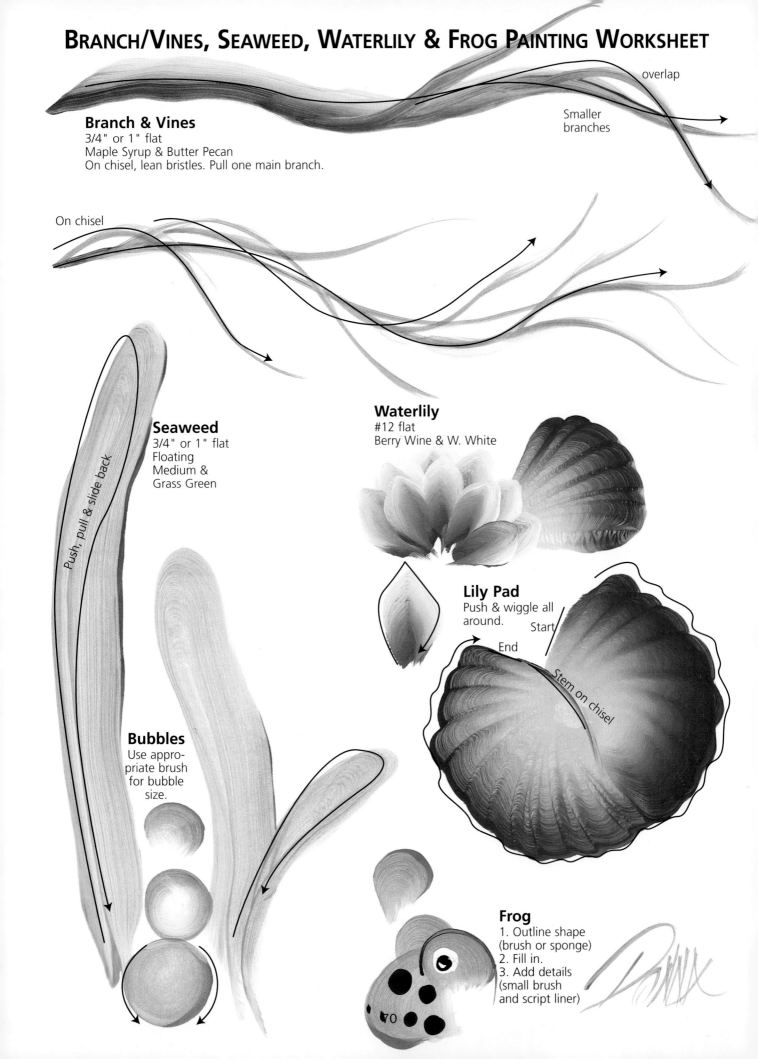

overlap

Smaller
branches

Branch & Vines
3/4" or 1" flat
Maple Syrup & Butter Pecan
On chisel, lean bristles. Pull one main branch.

On chisel

Push, pull & slide back

Seaweed
3/4" or 1" flat
Floating
Medium &
Grass Green

Waterlily
#12 flat
Berry Wine & W. White

Lily Pad
Push & wiggle all
around.

Start

End

Stem on chisel

Bubbles
Use appro-
priate brush
for bubble
size.

Frog
1. Outline shape
(brush or sponge)
2. Fill in.
3. Add details
(small brush
and script liner)

70

FEATHER, MOSS & WISTERIA PAINTING WORKSHEET

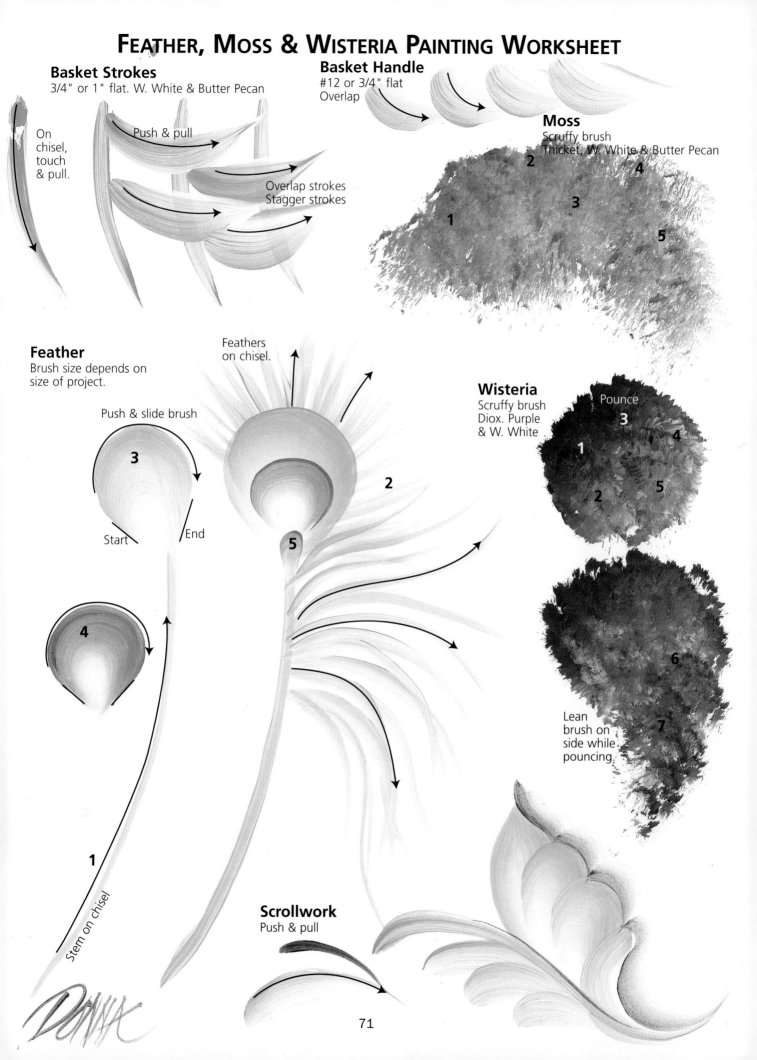

Basket Strokes
3/4" or 1" flat. W. White & Butter Pecan

On chisel, touch & pull.

Push & pull

Overlap strokes
Stagger strokes

Basket Handle
#12 or 3/4" flat
Overlap

Moss
Scruffy brush
Thicket, W. White & Butter Pecan

2   4
3
1   5

Feather
Brush size depends on size of project.

Feathers on chisel.

Push & slide brush

3
Start   End

4

5

2

1

Stem on chisel

Wisteria
Scruffy brush
Diox. Purple & W. White

Pounce
3
1   4
2   5

6

7

Lean brush on side while pouncing.

Scrollwork
Push & pull

71

ANGELFISH & EYES PAINTING WORKSHEET

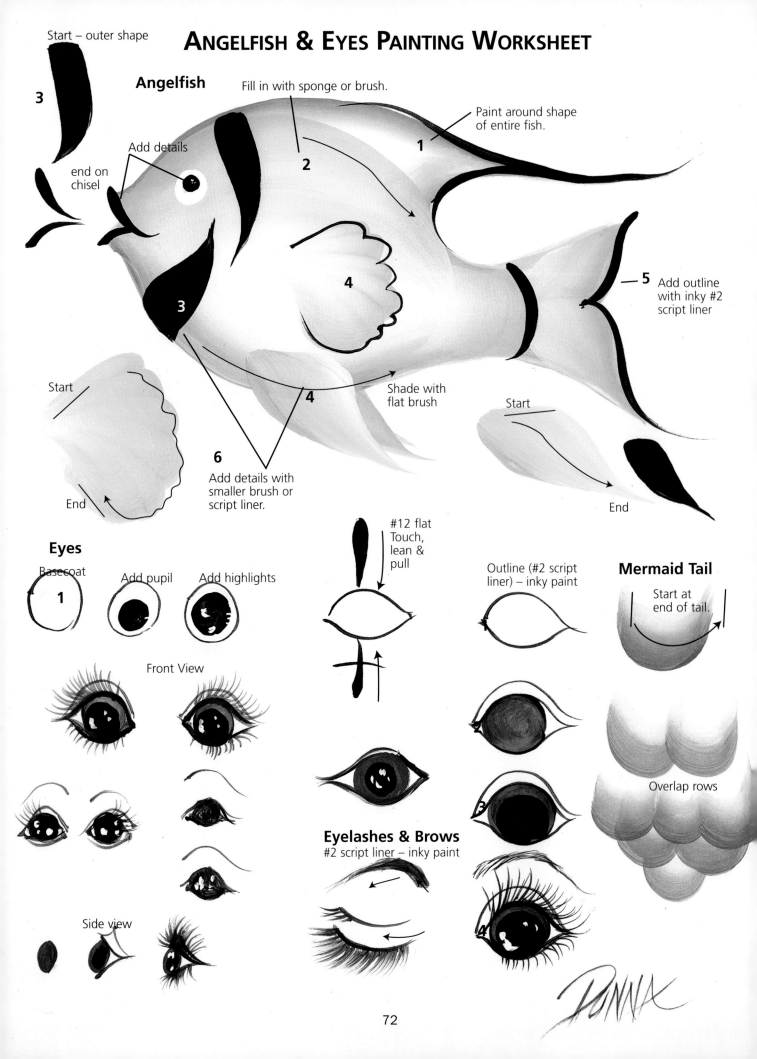

Angelfish

Start – outer shape

3

end on chisel

Add details

Fill in with sponge or brush.

Paint around shape of entire fish.

1

2

3

4

5 Add outline with inky #2 script liner

Start

End

6

4

Shade with flat brush

Add details with smaller brush or script liner.

Start

End

Eyes

Basecoat

1

Add pupil

Add highlights

Front View

Side view

#12 flat Touch, lean & pull

Outline (#2 script liner) – inky paint

Eyelashes & Brows
#2 script liner – inky paint

Mermaid Tail

Start at end of tail.

Overlap rows

72

DRAGONFLY PAINTING WORKSHEET

Wings
#12 Wicker White
Touch, lean, push, pull

Body
#12 Hunter Green/Cobalt

#2 Script Liner
Inky Hunter Green
or Black

Outline
#2 Script Liner
Inky Black

Tails
#2 Script Liner
Inky Hunter Green

GATHER THESE SUPPLIES

FolkArt® Acrylic Colors:
Basil Green 645
Butter Pecan 939
Engine Red 436
Fuchsia 635
Grass Green 644
Green Forest 448
Licorice 938
Light Fuchsia 688
Night Sky 443
School Bus Yellow 736
Skintone 949
Sunflower 432
Thicket 924
Wicker White 901

FolkArt® Acrylic Metallic & Sparkle Colors:
Blue Pearl 670 (Metallic)
Blue Sapphire 656 (Metallic)
Blue Topaz 651 (Metallic)
Champagne 675 (Metallic)
Iridescent Pearl 255 (Sparkles)
Peach Pearl 674 (Metallic)
Rose Pearl 673 (Metallic)
Rose Shimmer 652 (Metallic)

FolkArt® Artists' Pigment™ Colors:
Brilliant Ultramarine 484
Burnt Sienna 943
Dioxazine Purple 463
Pure Orange 628
Yellow Light 918
Yellow Ochre 917

FolkArt® One Stroke™ Brushes:
Flats – sizes #6, #12, 3/4", and 1"
Script liner – size #2
Scruffy brush

Painting Surfaces:
• Pre-painted Walls (Use egg-shell or satin latex wall paint as a base for your decorative painting. (In room pictured, the waves are painted with Behr® Premium Plus Colors in four colors of blue: "Ghost Blue" [closest to ceiling], "Island Sky" [next down], "Stratosphere" [next down], and "Moth Wing" [closest to floor].)

Continued on next page

Supplies (Cont.)
- Vinyl flooring for floorcloths (You will use the backside of vinyl flooring to paint floor-cloth. Canvas can also be used to make floorcloth. Enlarge patterns to the size desired to make floorcloths)
- Wood chest, painted white
- Wood seahorse lamp base*
- Wood starfish peg-shelf*
- Wood fish chair*
- Wood mirror frame*
- Octopus wood cutout* (in back of chest)

Two wood angelfish cutouts*
* www.jmoriginalcreations.com

Other Supplies:
FolkArt® One Stroke™ Sponge Painters 1195
FolkArt® Floating Medium 868

Painted Wall Scene

PREPARATION

1. Paint the walls with three tones of blues in a wave pattern. Start with the darker shade at the bottom, then paint middle section with a lighter shade of blue, and finally paint top section with an even lighter shade.
2. Place and outline your mermaid, fishes, treasure chest, and castle where you would desire them to be. Transfer or sketch any other patterns needed, such as seagrass and fish.

PAINT THE DESIGN

Angelfish:
Refer to "Angelfish & Eyes" Painting Worksheet, using colors given below.
1. Load the 1" flat brush with Floating Medium and sideload with a touch of Licorice. Add shading to upper fin, lower back fin, and face.
2. Load the 1" flat brush with Yellow Light. Add shading to tail, front fin, and body.
3. Load the #12 flat brush with Licorice. Paint stripes and eye. Allow to dry.
4. Load the #2 script liner with Licorice. Paint outer eye outline. Load the #2 script liner with Wicker White. Add highlights to eye.

5. Load the #12 flat brush with Engine Red. On chisel edge, touch and pull lips on fish.

Seagrass:
Refer to "Branch/Vines, Seaweed, Waterlily & Frog" Painting Worksheet, using colors given below.
Double load the 1" flat brush with Grass Green and Yellow Light. On chisel edge, leading with Yellow Light, touch, lean and pull blades to form seagrass.

Treasure Chest:
1. SAND: Dip dampened sponge into Wicker White and Butter Pecan. Make long smooth strokes with sponge to create sand. Rub edge of sponge into Butter Pecan. Add shading.

2. BEGIN CHEST: Dip a dampened sponge painter into Basil Green and Wicker White. Base coat chest. Allow to dry.
3. Load the 1" brush with Floating Medium and Thicket. Add outer shading on chest.
4. With same loaded brush, paint plaid on side of chest.
5. Load the #12 flat brush with Floating Medium and sideload with Thicket. Paint handles, lock, and leaf motif on front of trunk.
6. BEGIN JEWELS AND PEARLS: Load the #12 flat brush with Wicker White. Paint white pearls to fill the inside of trunk. Once white pearls are done, sideload a touch of Yellow

Ochre and add some shading to some of the pearls and jewels.

7. Double load the #12 flat brush with Yellow Ochre and Sunflower. On chisel edge, leading with Sunflower, paint tiara.

8. Double load the #12 flat brush with Wicker White and Brilliant Ultramarine. Paint jewels on tiara.

9. Using same brush with Brilliant Ultramarine to outer edge, paint blue string of pearls.

10. Load the #6 flat brush with Engine Red. Paint the ruby-like ring. Load the #2 script liner with Yellow Ochre. Paint gold on ring.

Mermaid:

1. Dip a dampened sponge painter into Skintone and a touch of metallic Peach Pearl. Fill in face arms and upper body of mermaid.

2. Dip dampened sponge painter into Brilliant Ultramarine and a touch of Wicker White and some metallic blue sapphire. With Brilliant Ultramarine to outer edge, fill in lower part of body.

3. SCALES ON LOWER BODY: Load the 1" flat brush with Floating Medium and sideload into Wicker White. Paint "C" strokes to form scales. *Refer to "Angelfish & Eyes" Painting Worksheet, using colors given here.*

4. Load the 1" flat brush with Wicker White and a touch of Light Fuchsia. On chisel edge, leading with Wicker White, add details to tail.

5. HAIR: Load the 1" flat brush with Burnt Sienna alternating with Yellow Ochre. On chisel edge, start at top of forehead and pull strokes to form hair. Make sure you pick up a touch of Floating Medium on brush to make long wavy strokes to form hair. Make darker strokes around hairline.

6. BEGIN FACIAL FEATURES: Load the 3/4" flat brush with Floating Medium and sideload Skintone. With Skintone to outer edge, add definition to facial features and details to arms.

7. EYE: Load the #12 flat brush with Wicker White. Paint white of eye. Allow to dry. Load the #6 flat brush with Wicker White and Brilliant Ultramarine. Work in colors to create a nice shade of blue. Paint iris part of eye. *Refer to "Angelfish & Eyes" Painting Worksheet, using colors given here.*

8. Load the #2 script liner with inky Burnt Sienna. Paint eyebrow, outline eye, and paint eyelashes.

9. Load the #6 flat brush with Engine Red. Using a touch-lean-and-pull stroke, paint lips.

10. SHELL SWIM TOP: Double load the 1" flat brush with Light Fuchsia, a touch of Wicker White, and metallic Peach Pearl. With Light Fuchsia to outer edge, push brush so bristles are spread and wiggle back and forth to form the shell-like shape.

11. With same loaded brush, paint starfish on mermaid's hand.

12. Double load the 3/4" flat brush with School Bus Yellow and Green Forest. On chisel edge, leading with School Bus Yellow, paint vine. Start on side of shell and pull toward body. Paint One Stroke leaves by pushing, turning and pulling back to chisel edge. *Refer to "Leaves & Cattail" Painting Worksheet, using colors given here.*

Continued on next page

13. With same loaded brush, paint seaweed on starfish. *Refer to "Branch/Vines, Seaweed, Waterlily & Frog" Painting Worksheet, using colors given here.*

14. BUBBLES AROUND MERMAID: These bubbles are a combination of various colors. Start by loading 1" flat brush for bigger bubbles and alternating with sizes 3/4", #12, and #6 brushes for smaller bubbles. Load brush with Floating Medium then sideload into Wicker White alternating with Brilliant Ultramarine and occasionally sideloading metallic Blue Sapphire or metallic Blue Topaz, metallic Blue Pearl, and occasionally picking up a touch of Iridescent Pearl Sparkles. Have fun painting these bubbles. *Refer to "Branch/Vines, Seaweed, Waterlily & Frog" Painting Worksheet, using colors given here.*

Sandcastle:

1. Load the 1" flat brush with Floating Medium and Wicker White and sideload Butter Pecan. Paint sand castle with Butter Pecan to outer edge, following outline of castle, starting at top and working toward bottom.
2. For smaller sections, use the #12 flat brush.
3. Occasionally sideload metallic Champagne for highlights.

Pink & Orange Fish:

1. Load the 1" flat brush with metallic Rose Pearl. Paint faces.
2. Load the 1" flat brush with Rose Shimmer. Paint bodies. Allow to dry.
3. Double load the 1" flat brush with Wicker White and Pure Orange. With Pure Orange to outer edge, paint fins and tails, wiggling brush back and forth to create ripple effect.
4. LIPS: Load the #12 flat brush with Engine Red. Touch, lean and pull strokes to meet to form lips.
5. Load the #12 flat brush with Wicker White. Paint whites of eyes. Allow to dry.
6. Load the #2 script liner with inky Licorice. Outline eye and add pupil.
7. Load the #2 script liner with Wicker White. Add highlights on eye of each fish.

Green & Pink Fish:

1. Load the 1" flat brush with Grass Green. Paint body.
2. Load the 1" flat brush with Rose Shimmer. Paint fins and tail.
3. Load the 1" flat brush with Floating Medium and sideload into Green Forest. Add shading to body.

Seahorses:

1. Paint seahorses by instructions given for Seahorse Lamp.
2. Paint bubbles around seahorses the same as bubble around Mermaid.

Starfish:

Paint according to instructions given for Starfish Floorcloth.

Octopus:
Paint according to instructions given for Octopus Floorcloth.

Bubbles:
Paint bubbles on wall in various sizes using 3/4" flat and #12 flat brushes, following instructions for bubbles given for Sea Creature Mirror. ❑

Starfish Floorcloth

PREPARATION

1. Transfer pattern outline to vinyl and cut out floorcloth.
2. Basecoat with two coats of Wicker White (or equivalent color wall paint). Allow to dry after each coat.
3. Dip dampened sponge painter into Sunflower and paint starfish. Allow to dry.

PAINT THE DESIGN

1. Load the 1" flat brush with Floating Medium and sideload with School Bus Yellow. With School Bus Yellow to outer edge, paint outer shading around starfish.
2. Load the #12 flat brush with Wicker White. Basecoat eyeball. Allow to dry. Dip handle end of brush into Licorice. Dot eye.
3. Load the #2 script liner with inky Engine Red. Using tip of brush, paint mouth line. ❑

Starfish Peg Shelf

PREPARATION

1. Lightly sand and clean surface.
2. Basecoat with two coats of Wicker White. Allow to dry after each coat.
3. Load the 1" flat brush with Sunflower. Basecoat the starfish.

PAINT THE DESIGN

1. Paint the starfish according to instructions for starfish floorcloth.
2. Double load the scruffy brush with Wicker White and Night Sky. Pounce color on ends of pegs. ❑

Sea Creatures Mirror

PREPARATION

1. Lightly sand mirror frame and clean free of dust before basecoating.
2. Basecoat frame with two coats of Wicker White, allowing to dry after each coat. Also sand lightly before applying each coat.

PAINT THE DESIGN

Pink Fish:

1. Double load the 1" flat brush with Fuchsia and a touch Wicker White. Work paint into brush for a nice soft shade of Fuchsia. Paint fish. Allow to dry.
2. Load the 1" flat brush with Floating Medium and sideload into Fuchsia. With Fuchsia to outer edge, paint shading on outer edge of fish. Paint body outline.
3. Load the #12 flat brush with Wicker White. Paint white circle of eye. Allow to dry. Dip handle end of brush into Licorice. Dot eye.

Starfish:

Paint according to instructions given for Starfish Floorcloth.

Seahorse:

Paint according to instructions given for Seahorse Lamp.

Orange Fish:

Paint according to instructions for Fish Floorcloth.

Bubbles:

Refer to "Branch/Vines, Seaweed, Waterlily & Frog" Painting Worksheet, using colors given below.

Load the #12 flat brush with Floating Medium and sideload into Brilliant Ultramarine. With Brilliant Ultramarine to outer edge, making full circles while pivoting on one side of brush, paint bubbles. For a variety of bubbles, sideload with Wicker White and follow above directions. You may also want to pick up a touch of Iridescent Pearl Sparkles for a different look. ❑

Octopus Wood Cutout & Chest

PREPARATION

1. Lightly sand wood cutout and clean free of dust before basecoating.
2. Basecoat cutout and wood chest with two coats of Wicker White (or equivalent color wall paint), allowing to dry after each coat. Also sand lightly before applying each coat.

PAINT THE DESIGN

1. Paint the octopus by instructions given for Octopus Floorcloth.
2. Position chest in front of octopus cutout hung on the wall. Transfer octopus arms pattern. Paint by the same octopus instructions, so that it appears that octopus' arms spill onto chest for a 3D effect. Refer to photo of project. ❑

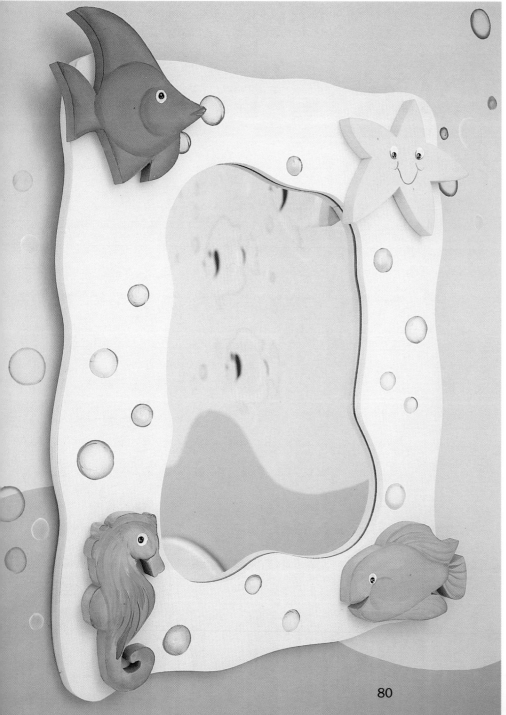

Seahorse Lamp

PREPARATION

1. Lightly sand and clean lamp free of dust before basecoating.
2. Basecoat lamp base and seahorse with two coats of Wicker White, allowing to dry after each coat. Also sand lightly before applying each coat.
3. Dip a moistened sponge into Night Sky. Using a paper towel, blot off excess paint. Lightly pounce sponge on base of lamp and shade.
4. Double load the 1" flat brush with Wicker White and Night Sky. With Wicker White turned toward the bottom, wash the feet of the lamp, using a back and forth motion.

PAINT THE DESIGN

1. Double load the 1" flat brush with Grass Green and Wicker White. Paint body of seahorse.
2. Load the 1" flat brush with Floating Medium and Grass Green. Add outer shading to body. Also add cheek.
3. With same loaded brush, on chisel edge, pull strokes downward to paint scales, picking up a touch of School Bus Yellow and Grass Green as you work.
4. Load the #12 flat brush with Wicker White. Paint eye. Allow to dry. Dip handle end of brush into Licorice. Dot eye. ❑

Octopus Floorcloth

PREPARATION

1. Transfer pattern outline to vinyl and cut out floorcloth.
2. Basecoat with two coats of Wicker White (or equivalent color wall paint). Allow to dry after each coat.
3. Dip a dampened sponge into Wicker White and Dioxazine Purple. Cover entire octopus.

PAINT THE DESIGN

1. Load the 1" flat brush with Floating Medium and sideload into Dioxazine Purple. With Dioxazine Purple to outer edge, add shading to outer edge of octopus body.
2. With same loaded brush, add cheeks.
3. Load the 3/4" flat brush with Floating Medium and sideload into Dioxazine Purple. Add spots to tentacles. (For

82

Octopus Floorcloth (cont.)

smaller spots, use the #12 flat brush.)

4. Load the 3/4" flat brush with Wicker White and paint eyes. Allow to dry. Load the #12 flat brush with Licorice and paint inner eyes.

5. Load the #2 script liner with inky Licorice. Paint eyebrows and smile.

6. Load the #2 script liner with Wicker White. Add eye highlights. ❑

Fish Chair

PREPARATION

1. Lightly sand and clean debris from surface of chair.

2. Basecoat with two coats of Wicker White (or equivalent color of wall paint). Allow to dry after each coat.

3. Load the scruffy brush with Wicker White and Night Sky. Pounce color on seat, creating a faux finish effect.

PAINT THE DESIGN

1. Double load the 1" flat brush with Pure Orange and Wicker White. Work colors into brush to create a nice rich orange color. Basecoat fish. Allow to dry.

2. Paint legs with same brush and color.

3. Paint the details on fish according to instructions for fish floorcloth.

4. Double load the 1" flat brush with Wicker White and Fuchsia. Work colors into brush to create a nice rich pink color. Paint ball feel and back dowels of chair. ❑

Fish Floorcloth

PREPARATION

1. Transfer pattern outline to vinyl and cut out floorcloth.
2. Basecoat with two coats of Wicker White (or equivalent color wall paint). Allow to dry after each coat.
3. Dip dampened sponge painter into Pure Orange and Wicker White and paint fish. Allow to dry.

PAINT THE DESIGN

1. Load the 1" flat brush with Floating Medium and sideload with Pure Orange. With Pure Orange to outer edge, paint outer shading on body and cheek.
2. With same loaded brush on chisel edge, paint stripes on fins and tail. Add inner body shading.
3. Load the #12 flat brush with Wicker White. Paint eye. Allow to dry. Dip handle end of brush into Licorice and dot eye.
4. Load the #2 script liner with Engine Red. Add shading to mouth area. ❑

Patterns

Enlarge Patterns at % given or to size needed.

Green and Pink Fish
240%

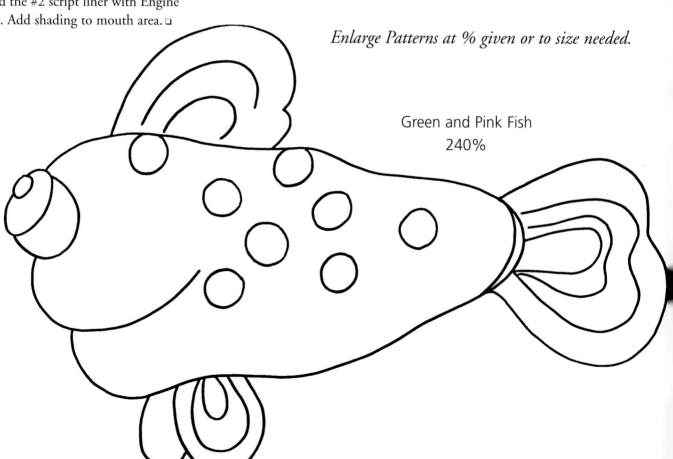

Patterns

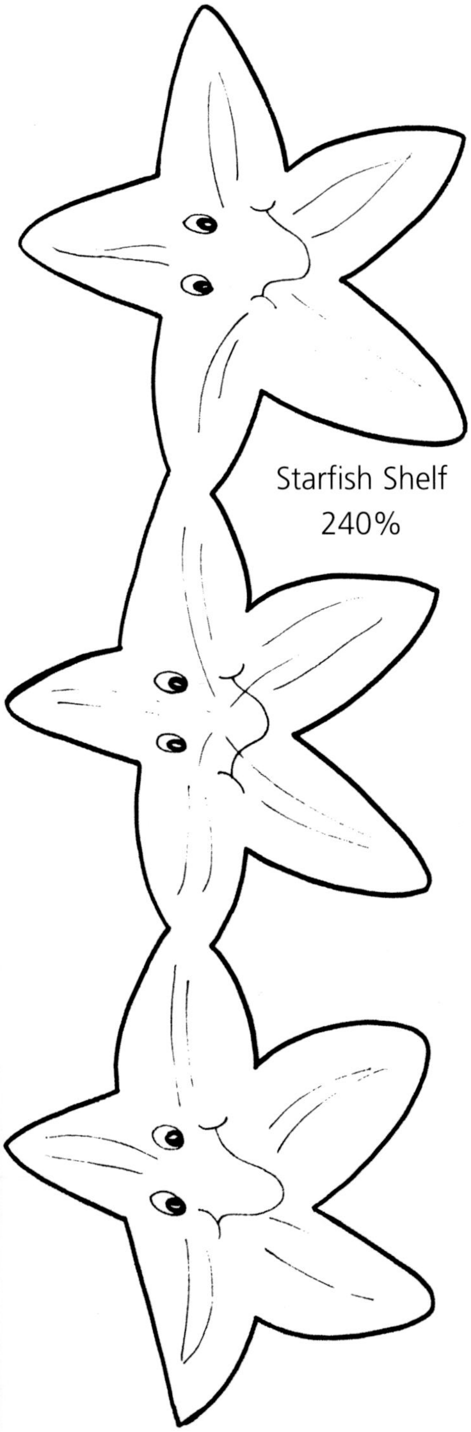

Starfish Shelf
240%

Mermaid
600%

Patterns

Starfish on Wall

Seahorse –
Wall & Lamp
170%

Fish

Patterns

Treasure Chest
240%

*Enlarge Patterns at % given
or to size needed.*

Patterns

*Enlarge Patterns at % given
or to size needed.*

Black & Yellow Fish
235%

Pink Fish
230%

Patterns

Fish Floorcloth
350%

Patterns

Octopus
Floorcloth
320%

Patterns

Starfish
Floorcloth
450%

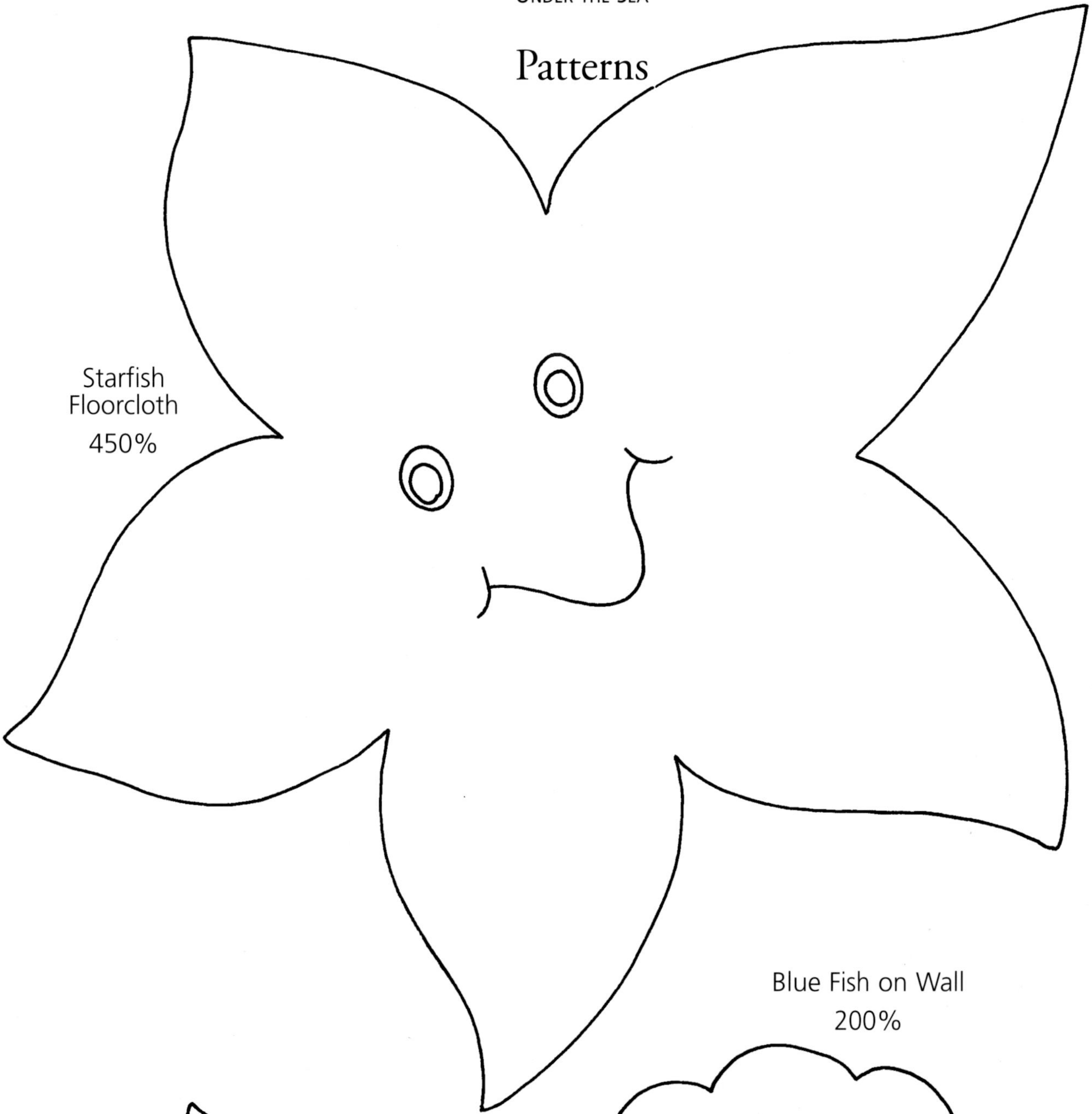

Blue Fish on Wall
200%

Mirror
200%

Sand Castle
450%

Dresser & Wall
Cutout
530%

Back of Dresser

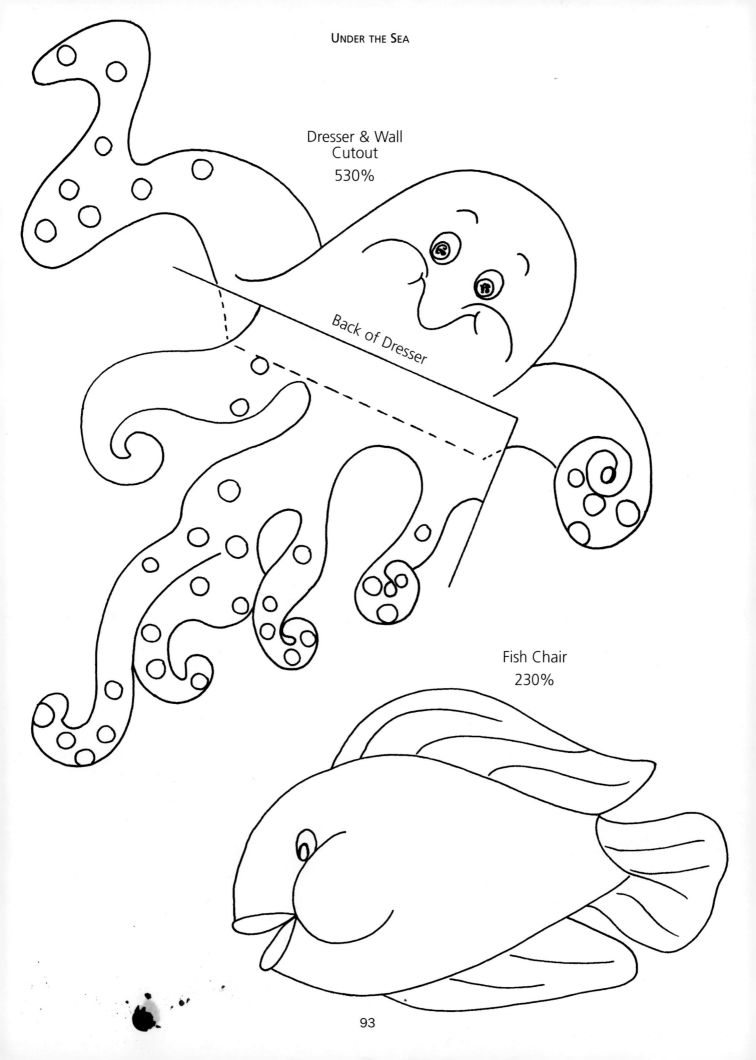

Fish Chair
230%

TOPIARIES & SCROLLS
Painted Wall Designs

GATHER THESE SUPPLIES

FolkArt® Acrylic Colors:
Butter Pecan 939
Green Forest 448
Maple Syrup 945
Sunflower 432
Thicket 924
Wicker White 901

FolkArt® One Stroke™ Brushes:
Flats – sizes #12 and 1"
Script liner – size #2
Large scruffy brush

Painting Surfaces:
Pre-painted Walls (Use a satin or egg-shell latex wall paint. This was is painted a taupe color.)

Other Supplies:
FolkArt® One Stroke™ Sponge Painters 1195
FolkArt® Floating Medium 868

PREPARATION

1. Clean wall thoroughly in areas to be painted.
2. Transfer urn and scroll patterns on wall.

PAINT THE DESIGN

Topiaries:

1. Dip a dampened sponge painter into Wicker White and Butter Pecan. Using straight side of sponge, with Wicker White to outer edge, paint outline of urns (paint one urn at the time). Then using a circular motion, pull paint from edges toward center to fill in.
2. To paint details, you can use the flat or round end of sponge, as needed, with same colors.
3. Load the 1" flat brush with Floating Medium and sideload into Wicker White. With Wicker White to outer edge, add shading and details.
4. For center urn, transfer embossed rose pattern. Load the 1" flat brush with Floating Medium, then load with Butter Pecan and sideload with Wicker White. With Wicker White to outer edge, paint roses and leaves.
5. Double load the 1" flat brush with Butter Pecan and Maple Syrup. On chisel edge, leading with Butter Pecan, paint topiary trunks.
6. Multi load the large scruffy brush with Thicket, Butter Pecan, a touch of Sunflower, and a touch of Maple Syrup on the Thicket side. Pounce moss on urns and a little on bottom to give the effect of spilled moss.
7. With same loaded brush, paint topiary greenery, adding Green Forest on Thicket side to add shading and definition between topiaries.

Continued on page 97

Continued from page 94

8. Load the #12 flat brush with Floating Medium and Thicket, occasionally picking up a touch of Maple Syrup. On chisel edge, paint vine and one stroke leaves, wrapping around three-ball topiary. *Refer to "Leaves & Cattail" Painting Worksheet, using colors given here.*

9. Tendrils: Load the #2 script liner with inky Thicket. Add curliques.

Over Door and Window Scrollwork:
Note: In this room, walls were painted with a taupe shade. Therefore, the white was placed to the outer edge to achieve the depth of the painting. If painting on a lighter color wall, reverse the colors.

1. Load the 1" flat brush with Floating Medium and double load with Wicker White and Butter Pecan. With Wicker White to outer edge, start painting scroll working strokes from extreme edges toward center. Important: The way you layer the strokes is what gives that 3-D look. ❑

Patterns

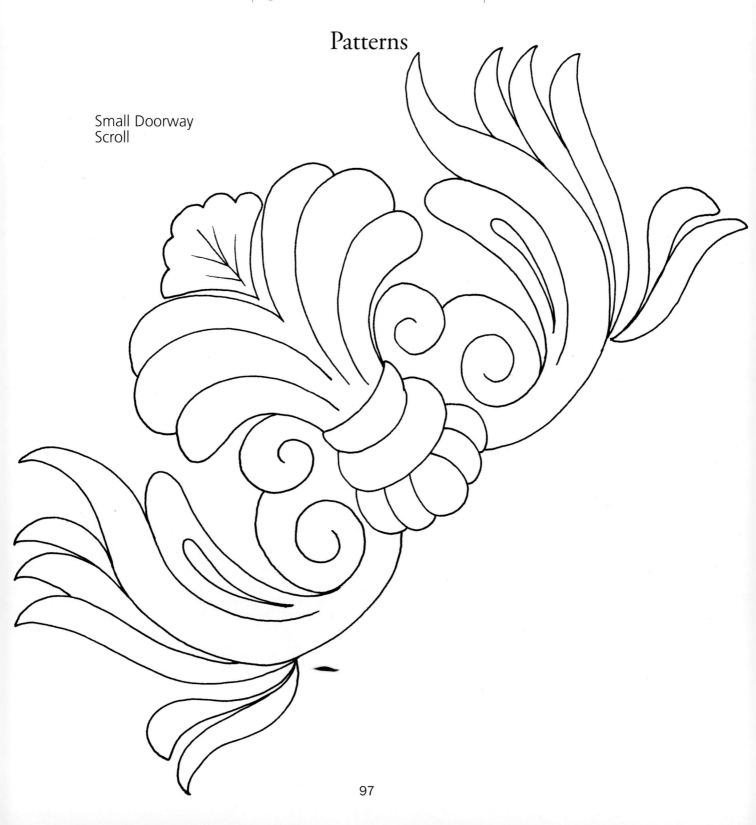

Small Doorway
Scroll

Patterns

center

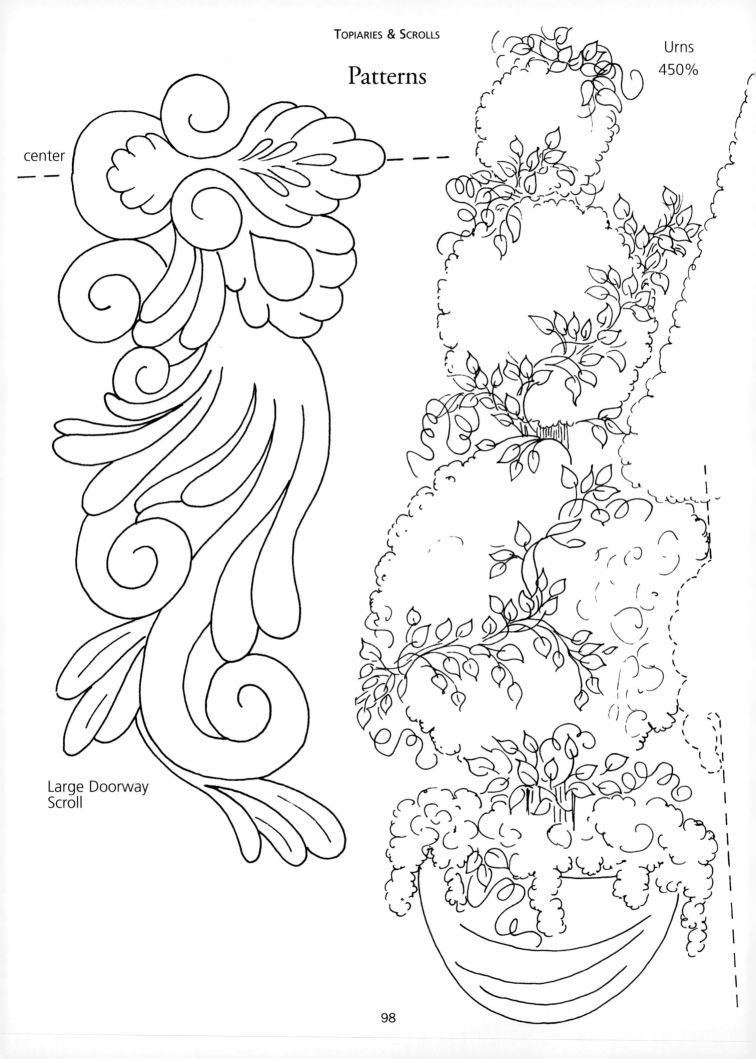

Large Doorway
Scroll

Patterns

*Enlarge Patterns at % given
or to size needed.*

Connect patterns at dotted lines

99

BOUQUETS & PLAID

GATHER THESE SUPPLIES

FolkArt® Acrylic Colors:
Basil Green 645
Fuchsia 635
Grass Green 644
Italian Sage 467
Licorice 938
Linen 420
Thicket 924
Wicker White 901

FolkArt® Artists' Pigment™ Colors:
Alizarin Crimson 758
Pure Magenta 689

FolkArt® One Stroke™ Brushes:
Flats – sizes #2, #6, #12, 3/4", 1", and 1-1/2"
Script liner – size #2

Painting Surfaces:
• Pre-painted Walls (Use eggshell or satin finish latex wall paint as a base for your decorative painting. This wall is painted an off-white color.)
• Old wood desk
• Wood blanket chest*
• Wood bouquet/ribbon cutout

and shadow boxes*
• Trio of three wood frames (includes wall mirror frame and two small photo frames)*
• Wood lamp with flower cluster cutout*
* www.jmoriginalcreations.com

Other Supplies:
FolkArt® One Stroke™ Sponge Painters 1195
FolkArt® Floating Medium 868
Royal Coat® Decoupage Foil Kit 1422 (or gold metal leafing)

Painted Wall Designs

PREPARATION
Transfer patterns to walls.

PAINT THE DESIGN

Red Roses:
Refer to "Flower" Painting Worksheet #1, using colors given below.

1. Double load the 1" flat brush with Alizarin Crimson and Wicker White, sideloading a touch of Pure Magenta on Alizarin Crimson side. With Alizarin Crimson to outer edge, paint five or six shell-like petals to form outer skirt of rose. Paint these petals by pushing on bristles and, while pivoting on Wicker White side, wiggle bristles until you create a shell-like petal. Overlap petals.
2. Paint a rosebud for center of each rose as shown on the Painting Worksheet.
3. Starting on side of rosebud, paint second row of shell-like petals.
4. Re-stroke rosebud to clean up strokes.
5. On chisel edge, starting on sides of rosebuds, paint center strokes as shown on the Painting Worksheet.

Chrysanthemums:
Refer to "Flower" Painting Worksheet #2, using colors given below.

Continued on page 102

Continued from page 100

1. Double load the 1" flat brush with Alizarin Crimson and Linen, occasionally sideloading a touch of Pure Magenta on the Alizarin Crimson side. With Alizarin Crimson to outer edge, paint five or six shell-like petals to form outer skirt of each flower. You paint these petals by pushing on bristles and, while pivoting on Wicker White side, wiggle bristles until you create a shell-like petal. Overlap petals.

2. With Alizarin Crimson to outer edge, on chisel edge and starting at center, touch, lean, and pull stroke to center of flower. Repeat same strokes on each side of center stroke, becoming smaller as you get farther away from center. Repeat second and third row. Refer to Painting Worksheet.

Pink Flower Clusters

Refer to "Flower" Painting Worksheet #1, using colors given below.

1. SMALLER PINK FLOWERS: Double load the #12 flat brush with Fuchsia and Wicker White. With Fuchsia to outer edge, paint five-petal flowers. You paint these petals by pushing very hard on bristles and, while pivoting on Wicker White side, move brush back and forth until you create a shell-like petal. Overlap petals.

2. LARGER PINK FLOWERS: Load the 1" flat brush with Alizarin Crimson and Linen. With Linen to outer edge, paint five or six shell-like petals to form outer skirt of flower. You paint these petals by pushing on bristles and, while pivoting on Alizarin Crimson side, move brush back and forth until you create a shell-like petal. Overlap petals.

3. With same brush, paint two or three of these petals to form buds.

4. Load the #6 flat brush with Grass Green then sideload Wicker White. With Grass Green to outer edge, paint "C" strokes to form centers for both sizes of flowers.

Calyxes & Leaves:

Refer to "Leaves & Cattail" Painting Worksheet, using colors given below.

1. Double load the 1" flat brush with Thicket and Basil Green. On chisel edge, touch and pull three or four strokes to form calyxes of buds.

2. With Basil Green to outer edge, paint wiggle leaves and one stroke leaves. Paint in the same manner as for shell-like petals, but go a little farther then lift up to chisel at point.

3. Load the #12 flat brush with Thicket and Basil Green. Paint small one stroke leaves. You paint these leaves by pushing, turning, and lifting back to chisel. Refer to Painting Worksheet. Allow to dry.

Black Outlining:

Load the #2 script liner with inky Licorice. Outline around flowers and leaves. ❏

Painted Desk

PREPARATION

1. Lightly sand and clean surface.

2. Basecoat with two coats of Italian Sage (or the equivalent color wall paint). Allow to dry.

3. Rub dampened sponge painter into Thicket. Antique edges all around desk using a circular motion, making sure that the edges are a little darker. Let dry.

4. Transfer patterns to desk.

PAINT THE DESIGN

Red Roses:

Paint according to red roses instructions given for walls.

Chrysanthemums:

Paint according to chrysanthemums instructions given for walls.

Pink Flower Clusters:

Paint according to pink flower clusters instructions given for walls.

Leaves:

Paint according to leaves instructions given for walls.

Black Outlining:

Load the #2 script liner with inky Licorice. Outline around flowers and leaves.

Plaid:

1. Load the 1" flat brush with Alizarin Crimson and Floating Medium. Paint red horizontal stripes approximately 1" apart. Paint vertical red stripes approximately 1" apart.

2. With same colors and same brush on chisel edge, paint thin vertical and horizontal stripes.

3. Load the 1" flat brush with Wicker White and Floating Medium. On chisel edge, paint additional vertical and horizontal stripes.

Wood Inserts Above Desk Legs:

1. Double load the 1" flat brush with Alizarin Crimson and Wicker White. Basecoat insert areas. Allow to dry.

2. Double load the #12 flat brush with Wicker White and Thicket. On chisel edge, leading with Wicker White, paint crosshatch pattern. With brush on chisel, at each intersection where the lines cross, touch and pull small teardrop stroke.

Tassels:

1. Double load the #12 flat brush with Alizarin Crimson and Wicker White. With Alizarin Crimson to outer edge, paint "C" strokes to form top part of each tassel.

2. With brush on chisel edge and leading with Wicker White, paint fringe on tassel. To add shading, turn brush around and lead with Alizarin Crimson.

Gold Leafing or Foil:

Following manufacturer's instructions, add gold foil or gold leafing to all hardware and molding around routed edge. ❏

Shadow Boxes On Ribbon/ Bouquet Cutout

PREPARATION

1. Lightly sand and clean surfaces of wood cutout and shadow boxes.
2. Basecoat all pieces with two coats of Wicker White. Allow to dry.
3. Load the 1-1/2" flat brush with Italian Sage, picking up water as necessary to create a soft wash. Paint inside and outside of boxes.
4. Transfer flower pattern to cutout.

PAINT THE DESIGN

Plaid on Ribbon Cutout:

Paint according to instructions given for plaid blanket chest lid.

Floral Spray:

Paint according to instructions given for flowers on walls. ❏

Blanket Chest

PREPARATION

1. Lightly sand and clean surface.
2. Basecoat with two coats of Wicker White (or equivalent color wall paint). Allow to dry.
3. Rub a dampened sponge painter into Italian Sage, picking up water as necessary to create a soft wash, and color-wash chest. Let dry.
4. Paint lower trim of chest with Thicket and Floating Medium. Let dry. Load the 1" flat brush with Alizarin Crimson and paint ball feet. Let dry.
5. Transfer floral patterns to front and sides of chest.

PAINT THE DESIGN

Plaid (Chest Lid):

1. Load the 1-1/2" flat brush with Alizarin Crimson and Floating Medium. Paint red horizontal stripes approximately 2" apart. Paint vertical red stripes approximately 2" apart.
2. With same colors and same brush on chisel edge, paint thin vertical and horizontal stripes.
3. Load the 1" flat brush with Wicker White and Floating Medium. On chisel edge, paint additional vertical and horizontal stripes.
4. Load the 1" flat brush with Alizarin Crimson and Floating Medium. Paint red horizontal stripes approximately 1" apart. Paint vertical red stripes approximately 1" apart.
5. With same colors and same brush on chisel edge, paint thin vertical and horizontal stripes.
6. Load the 1" flat brush with Thicket and Floating Medium. On chisel edge, paint additional vertical and horizontal stripes.

Flower Cluster on Front:

Paint by the instructions given for flowers on walls and desk.

Flower Clusters on Sides:

1. LEAVES: Double load the 1" flat brush with Thicket and Basil Green. With Basil Green to outer edge, paint wiggle leaves and One Stroke leaves. Paint in the same manner as for shell-like petals, but go a little farther then lift up to chisel at point.

Continued on next page

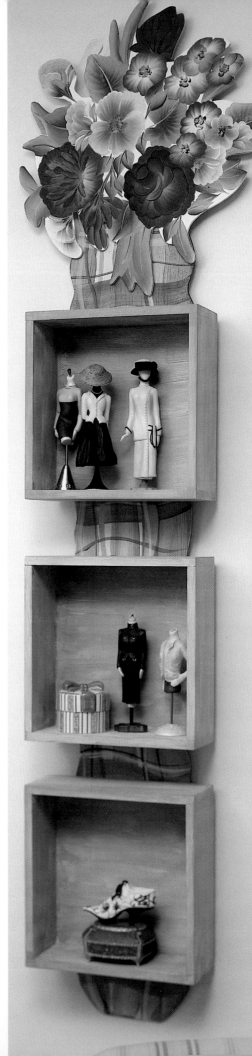

FLOWERS:

2. Double load the #12 flat brush with Fuchsia and Wicker White. With Fuchsia to outer edge, paint five-petal flowers. You paint these petals by pushing very hard on bristles and, while pivoting on Wicker White side, move brush back and forth until you create a shell-like petal. Overlap petals.

3. With same brush paint two to three of these petals to form buds.

4. Load the #6 flat brush with Grass Green then sideload Wicker White. With Grass Green to outer edge, paint "C" strokes to form flower centers.

5. CALYXES: Double load the 1" flat brush with Thicket and Basil Green. On chisel edge, touch and pull three to four strokes to calyxes of buds.

6. LEAVES: Load the #12 flat brush with Floating Medium and a touch of Thicket. Paint small one stroke leaves. Paint these leaves by pushing, turning, and lifting back to chisel. *Refer to "Leaves & Cattail" Painting Worksheet, using colors given here.*

Black Outlining:

Load the #2 script liner with inky Licorice. Outline around flowers and leaves. ❑

Plaid Mirror & Photo Frames

PREPARATION

1. Lightly sand and clean surfaces.
2. Basecoat with two coats of Wicker White. Allow to dry.

PAINT THE DESIGN

1. Load the 3/4" or #12 flat brush (depending on size of frame you are currently working on) with Alizarin Crimson and Floating Medium. Paint red horizontal stripes. Paint vertical red stripes.
2. With same brush on chisel edge, paint thin vertical and horizontal stripes.
3. Load the #12 flat brush with Wicker White and Floating Medium. On chisel edge, paint additional vertical and horizontal stripes.
4. Load the #12 flat brush with Thicket and Floating Medium. On chisel edge, paint additional vertical and horizontal stripes. ❑

Flower Vase Lamp

PREPARATION

1. Lightly sand and clean surface.
2. Basecoat with two coats of Wicker White. Allow to dry.
3. Load the 1-1/2" flat brush with Italian Sage, picking up water as necessary to create a soft wash. Paint oval part of lamp and base. Refer to photo of project.
4. Load the 3/4" flat brush with Alizarin Crimson. Paint ball feet.
5. Transfer design wherever you will need a pattern.

PAINT THE DESIGN

Plaid:

1. Load the 1-1/2" or 1" flat brush (depending on size of plaid desired) with Alizarin Crimson and Floating Medium. Paint red horizontal stripes. Paint vertical red stripes.

2. With same brush on chisel edge, paint thin vertical and horizontal stripes.
3. Load the #12 flat brush with Wicker White and Floating Medium. On chisel edge, paint additional vertical and horizontal stripes.
4. Load the #12 flat brush with Thicket and Floating Medium. On chisel edge, paint additional vertical and horizontal stripes.

Floral spray:

Paint according to instructions given for flower clusters on wall. ❑

Patterns

Enlarge Patterns at % given or to size needed.

Mirror, Photo frames
195% for photo frames

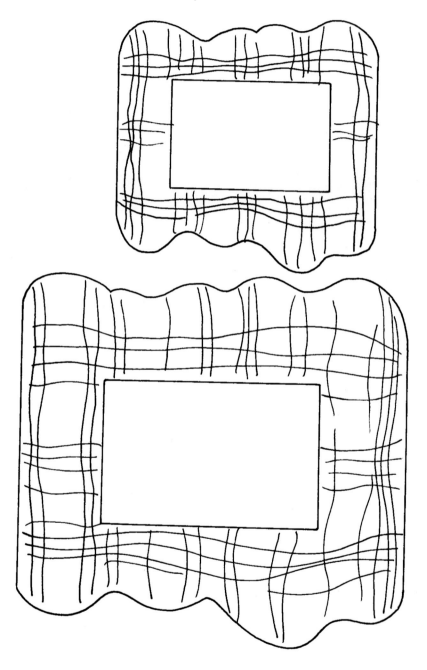

Patterns

Wood Cutout & Shadow Box

Wall, Blanket Chest: Trace elements
of design from cutout and desktop
to create floral patterns on
blanket chest and wall,
using photo as a guide.

205%

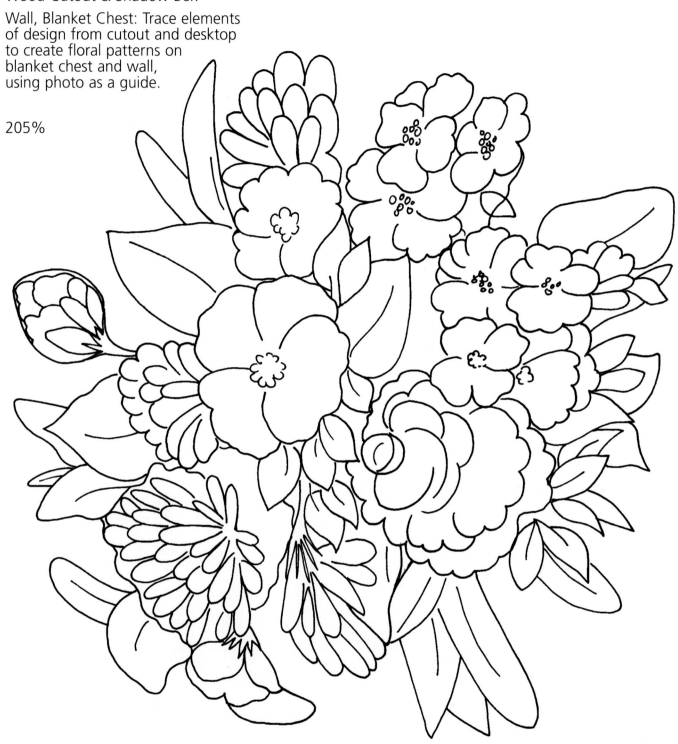

Lamp
200%

Patterns

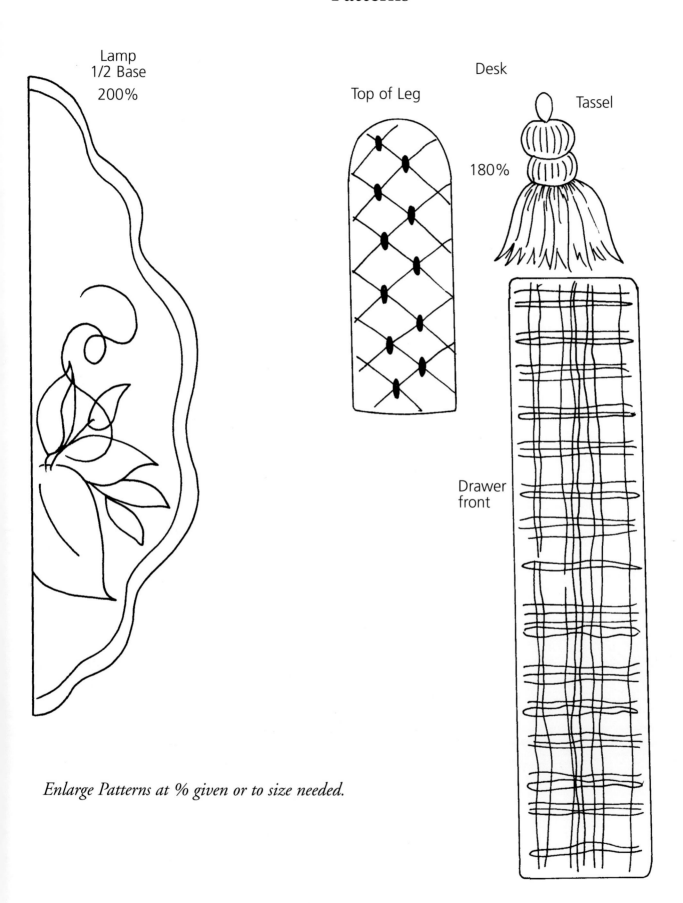

Lamp
1/2 Base
200%

Desk

Top of Leg

Tassel

180%

Drawer
front

Enlarge Patterns at % given or to size needed.

Patterns

Enlarge Patterns at % given or to size needed.

Desktop

For sides, refer to photo and
use floral elements from top.

300%

Connect at dotted lines to complete pattern

Patterns

BUNNIES IN THE GARDEN

GATHER THESE SUPPLIES

FolkArt® Acrylic Colors:
Butter Pecan 939
Dark Plum 469
Licorice 938
Midnight 964
Sunflower 432
Thicket 924
Wicker White 901

**FolkArt® Artists' Pigment™
Colors:**
Burnt Umber 462
Yellow Ochre 917

FolkArt® One Stroke™ Brushes:
Flats – sizes #6, #12, 3/4" and 1"
Script liner – size #2
Scruffy brush

Painting Surfaces:
• Pre-painted Walls (Use an
  eggshell or satin finish latex
  wall paint as a base for your
  decorative painting. The walls
  shown are painted a burgundy
  color.)

Other Supplies:
FolkArt® One Stroke™ Sponge
Painters 1195
FolkArt® Floating Medium 868

Painted Wall Designs

PREPARATION

1. Clean all surfaces where you will be painting.
2. Transfer patterns to walls.

PAINT THE DESIGN

White Bunny:

1. Load a dampened sponge painter with Wicker White. Basecoat bunny. Allow to dry.

Continued on page 116

Continued from page 114

2. Load the 1" flat brush with Floating Medium and sideload with Butter Pecan. Add shading and details to body as seen in the photo of project.

3. Load the scruffy brush with Wicker White and sideload a touch of Butter Pecan. Pounce tail.

4. Wash inner ear with Dark Plum

5. Basecoat eye areas with Wicker White. Let dry. Add large Licorice pupil, filling up most of eye area. Let dry. Highlight pupil with Wicker White. Shade around inner part of eye with Dark Plum. Outline eye and add lashes with inky Licorice, using the script liner. *Refer to "Angelfish & Eyes" Painting Worksheet.*

6. Paint whiskers with inky Wicker White, using the script liner.

Brown Bunny:

1. Load dampened sponge painter with Butter Pecan. Basecoat bunny. Allow to dry.

2. Load the 1" flat brush with Floating Medium and sideload into Burnt Umber. Add shading and details to body as seen in photo of project.

3. Load the scruffy brush with Burnt Umber and a touch of Butter Pecan. Pounce tail.

4. Wash inner ear with Dark Plum

5. Basecoat eye areas with Wicker White. Let dry. Add large Licorice pupil, filling up most of eye area. Let dry. Highlight pupil with Wicker White. Outline eye and add lashes with inky Licorice, using the script liner. *Refer to "Angelfish & Eyes" Painting Worksheet.*

6. Paint whiskers with inky Wicker White, using the script liner.

Vines & Leaves:

1. Double load the 1" flat brush with Wicker White and Burnt Umber. On chisel edge, leading with Wicker White, paint vines and branches.

2. Double load the 1" flat brush with Thicket and Wicker White; occasionally picking up a touch of Butter Pecan on the Wicker White side or for a darker shade of leaf, pick up a touch of Burnt Umber on the Thicket side. On chisel edge and leading with Wicker White, paint grass blades around room.

3. With Thicket to outer edge, paint wiggle leaves and One Stroke leaves. *Refer to "Leaves & Cattail" Painting Worksheet.*

Flowers & Blueberries:

1. SMALL YELLOW/WHITE FLOWERS: Double load the #12 flat brush with Wicker White and Yellow Ochre. With Wicker White to outer edge, paint five individual

petals to form flowers.

2. Dip handle end of brush into Thicket and dot each flower center.

3. BLUEBERRIES: Double load the #6 flat brush with Midnight and a touch of Wicker White. With Midnight to outer edge, paint blueberries.

4. TENDRILS: Load the #2 script liner with inky Thicket. Paint curliques.

5. YELLOW/WHITE STALK FLOWERS: Double load the #12 flat brush with Wicker White and Yellow Ochre. Starting at tip of grass blade, with Wicker White to outer edge, paint teardrop shape strokes to form stalk flower as you work downward. *Refer to "Flowers" Painting Worksheet #2.*

6. HYDRANGEA: Double load the #12 flat brush with Wicker White and Dark Plum. With Wicker White to outer edge, paint the five-petal flowers, overlapping them slightly to create clusters to form hydrangea. Occasionally, you may turn Dark Plum to outer edge in some petals to give depth and shading. Dip handle end of brush into Sunflower. Dot centers.

Dragonflies:

Refer to "Critters" Painting Worksheet, using colors given below.

1. Load the 3/4" flat brush with Floating Medium and Wicker White. Paint wings.

2. Double load the #12 flat brush with Thicket and Midnight. Paint body by pushing and pulling brush to form body.

3. Load the #2 script liner with inky Thicket. Paint antennae.

Butterflies:

Refer to "Critters" Painting Worksheet, using colors given below.

1. Double load the #12 flat brush with Wicker White and Yellow Ochre. Paint wings.

2. Load the #2 script liner with inky Thicket. Paint body and antennae. □

Patterns

*Enlarge Patterns at % given
or to size needed.*

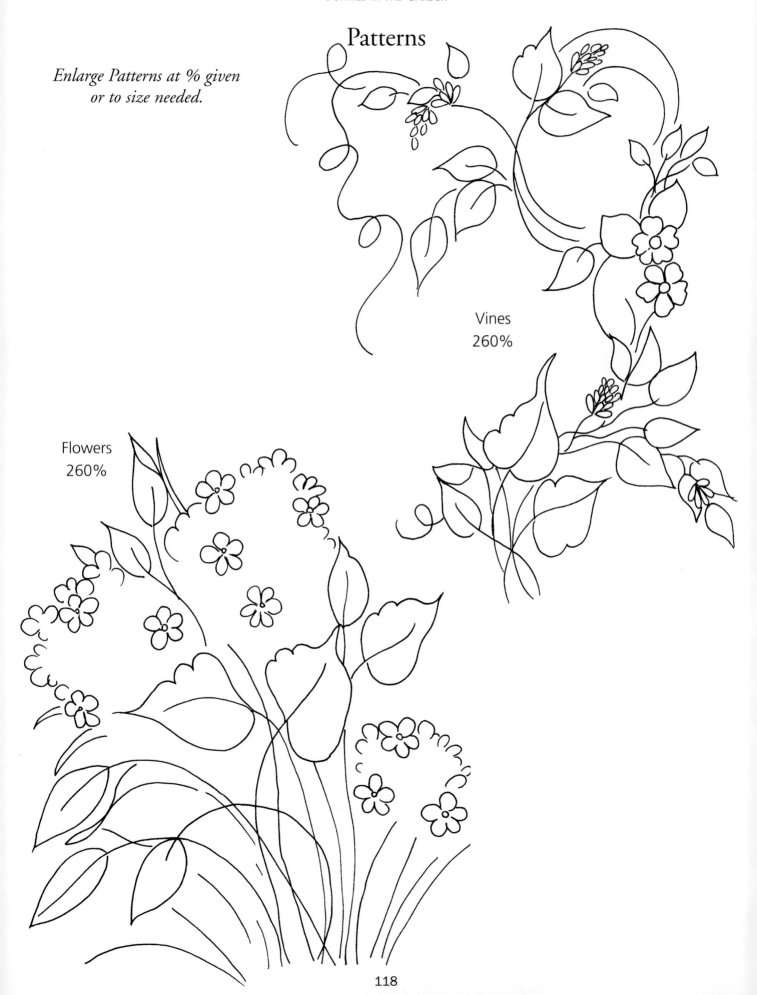

Vines
260%

Flowers
260%

Patterns

Vines
260%

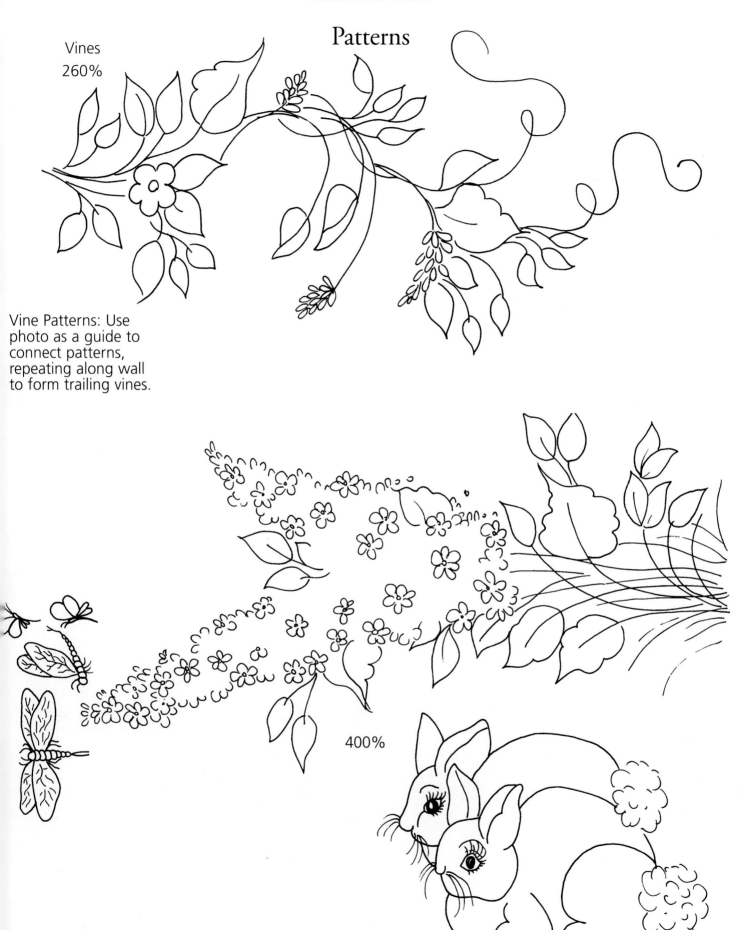

Vine Patterns: Use photo as a guide to connect patterns, repeating along wall to form trailing vines.

400%

PEACOCK FEATHERS

GATHER THESE SUPPLIES

FolkArt® Acrylic Colors:
Butter Pecan 939
Champagne 675 (Metallic)
Grass Green 644
Green Forest 448
Inca Gold 676 (Metallic)
Licorice 938
Peridot 671 (Metallic)
Sahara Gold 577 (Metallic)
Wicker White 901

FolkArt® Artists' Pigment™ Colors:
Alizarin Crimson 758
Dioxazine Purple 463
Pure Orange 628
Raw Umber 485

FolkArt® One Stroke™ Brushes:
Flats – sizes #12, 3/4" and 1"
Script liner – size #2

Painting Surfaces:
• Pre-painted Walls (Use an eggshell or satin finish latex wall paint as a base for your decorative painting. This room was painted a taupe or putty color that is the equivalent of FolkArt® Butter Pecan)
• Wood feather mirror frame*
• Wood feather shelf*
• Wood table*
• Wood feather picture frame*
* www.jmoriginalcreations.com

Other Supplies:
FolkArt® Floating Medium 868
Measuring tape
Painter's tape
Roller

Painted Walls

PREPARATION

1. Lightly sand and clean walls of any debris.
2. Transfer patterns to walls.

Continued on page 122

PAINT THE DESIGN

Stripes:

1. Depending on width of stripes desired, measure and tape off stripes. Refer to photo of project. After taping vertical stripes, tape off area for painting chair rail border.
2. Using a medium size roller, paint marked stripes with metallic Champagne Pearl. Pull off tape immediately after rolling paint. Allow to dry.

Feathers:

NOTES: These peacock feathers are painted on border, on walls, and on scroll design. Refer to "Feather, Moss & Wisteria" Painting Worksheet, using colors given below.

1. Double load the 1" flat brush with Wicker White and Butter Pecan. On chisel edge, leading with Wicker White, paint feather stems.
2. Keeping brush on chisel edge and leading with Wicker White, pull strokes from stem to form feather. Occasionally sideload a touch of metallic Sahara Gold alternating with metallic Peridot.
3. When each feather is finished, restroke its stem.
4. EYE OF FEATHER: Double load the 1" flat brush with Wicker White and Butter Pecan. With Butter Pecan to outer edge, paint first oval. Load the 3/4" flat brush with metallic Sahara Gold. Paint second oval. Load the #12 flat brush with metallic Peridot. Paint third oval. With the #12 flat brush loaded with Peridot, on chisel edge, paint additional small green feathers at bottom of eye. Refer to Painting Worksheet.

Scrollwork:

1. Double load the 1" flat brush with Wicker White and Butter Pecan, occasionally picking up a touch of metallic Sahara Gold. On chisel edge, first paint lattice-like strokes.
2. To paint leaves, turn Butter Pecan to outer edge, then touch, lean, and pull strokes toward main part of design. Work strokes from outside toward center of design.
3. Load the #12 flat brush with Wicker White and Butter Pecan. With Butter

Pecan to outer edge, paint circles.

4. To add depth and shading, load the 3/4" flat brush with Floating Medium and sideload Raw Umber. With Raw Umber toward design, paint shading. ▫

Peacock Feather Mirror

PREPARATION

1. Lightly sand and clean surface.
2. Basecoat with two coats of Licorice, allowing to dry after each coat.

PAINT THE DESIGN

Refer to "Feather, Moss & Wisteria" Painting Worksheet, using colors given below.

1. Load the 3/4" flat brush with Alizarin Crimson. Paint balls around edge. Sideload same loaded brush with Inca Gold. Add highlights to balls.
2. Double load the 1" flat brush with Dioxazine Purple and Wicker White. On chisel edge, leading with Wicker White, paint purple feathers around outer edge of mirror frame.
3. Double load the 1" flat brush with Green Forest and Grass Green. On chisel edge, leading with Grass Green, paint stems of feathers.
4. With same loaded brush, pull strokes from center of each stem outward to form each feather. Alternate picking up Peridot and Inca Gold. Work with these colors three-fourths of the way up into the feather.
5. Double load the 1" flat brush with Pure Orange and Wicker White; occasionally pick up a touch of Alizarin Crimson. On chisel edge, leading with Wicker White, paint upper part of each feather.
6. Load the 3/4" flat brush with Green Forest and Grass Green. Now sideload Peridot on the Green Forest side. Paint eye of each feather. Allow to dry. With same brush, leading with Grass Green, re-stroke each stem for a clean look.
7. Load the #12 flat brush with Alizarin Crimson. Paint inner ball of each feather's "eye." Now sideload Inca Gold and add highlights.

Continued on page 124

Peacock Mirror (cont.)

8. Load the #2 script liner with inky Licorice. Add outline around eye of each feather and a streak down each stem.

9. Load the 1" flat brush with Floating Medium and sideload Inca Gold. Stroke some gold on each stem and add shading around inner circle of mirror and wherever you want some gold highlights. ❑

Feather Shelf

PREPARATION

1. Lightly sand and clean surface.
2. Basecoat with two coats of Wicker White. Allow to dry after each coat.
3. Load 1" flat with Floating Medium and Peridot. Add a light wash to bottom of backboard below shelf and underside of shelf..
4. Transfer pattern to backboard of shelf.

PAINT THE DESIGN

Refer to "Feather, Moss & Wisteria" Painting Worksheet, using colors given below.

1. Double load the 1" flat brush with Wicker White and Butter Pecan. On chisel edge, leading with Wicker White, paint feather stems.

2. Keeping brush on chisel edge and pulling from stem, paint strokes to form each feather, occasionally sideloading a touch of metallic Sahara Gold alternately with metallic Peridot. When finished painting each feather, re-stroke stem.

3. Begin eye of feathers: Double load the 3/4" flat brush with Wicker White and Butter Pecan. With Butter Pecan to outer edge, paint first oval of each feather.

4. Load the #12 flat brush with metallic Sahara Gold. Paint second oval.

5. Load the #12 flat brush with metallic Peridot. Paint third oval.

6. Load the #12 flat brush with Peridot. On chisel edge, paint additional small green feathers at bottom of each eye. Refer to Painting Worksheet. ❑

Picture Frame

PREPARATION

1. Lightly sand and clean surface.
2. Basecoat with two coats of Wicker White. Allow to dry after each coat.
3. Transfer pattern to frame.

PAINT THE DESIGN

1. Paint feather by same instructions given for the Feather Shelf.

2. Paint border stripe around frame as seen in photo of project. Load the #2 script liner with Peridot. Paint one line leaning bristles down. Then paint a second line on top to create a thicker line. ❑

Feather Table

PREPARATION

1. Lightly sand and clean surface.
2. Basecoat with two coats of Wicker White (or equivalent color wall paint). Allow to dry after each coat.
3. Paint stripes on legs with metallic Peridot and Sahara Gold.
4. Transfer patterns to table.

PAINT THE DESIGN

Feathers:

Paint feathers by instructions given for Feather Shelf.

Scrollwork:

1. Load the 3/4" flat brush with Floating Medium and Peridot. On chisel edge, touch, lean, and pull strokes toward main design. ❑

Patterns

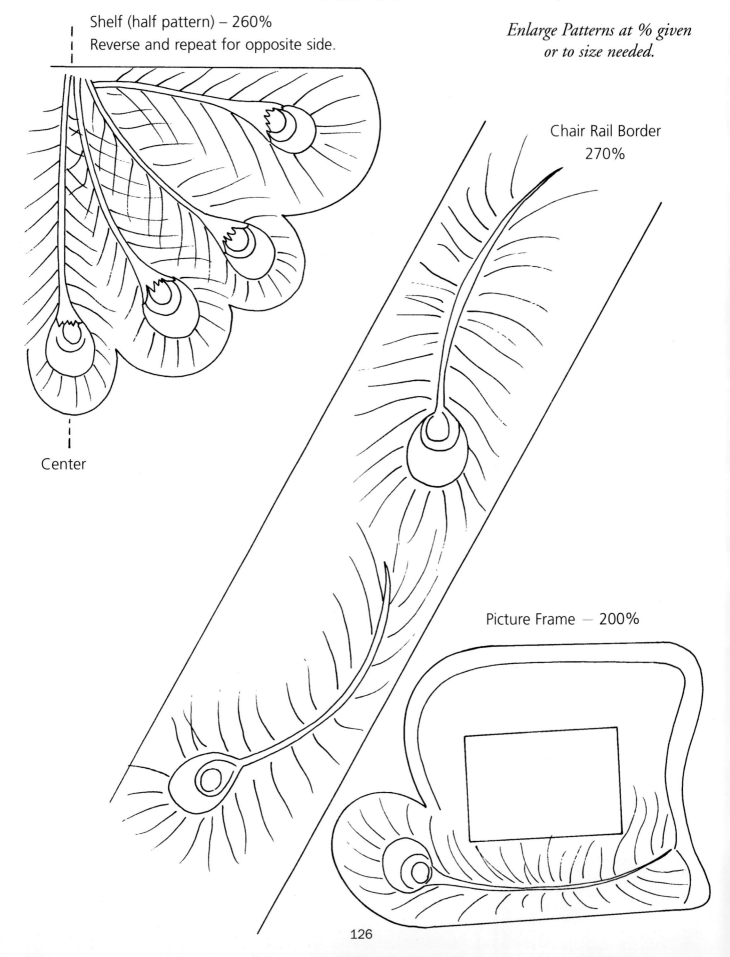

Shelf (half pattern) – 260%
Reverse and repeat for opposite side.

*Enlarge Patterns at % given
or to size needed.*

Center

Chair Rail Border
270%

Picture Frame — 200%

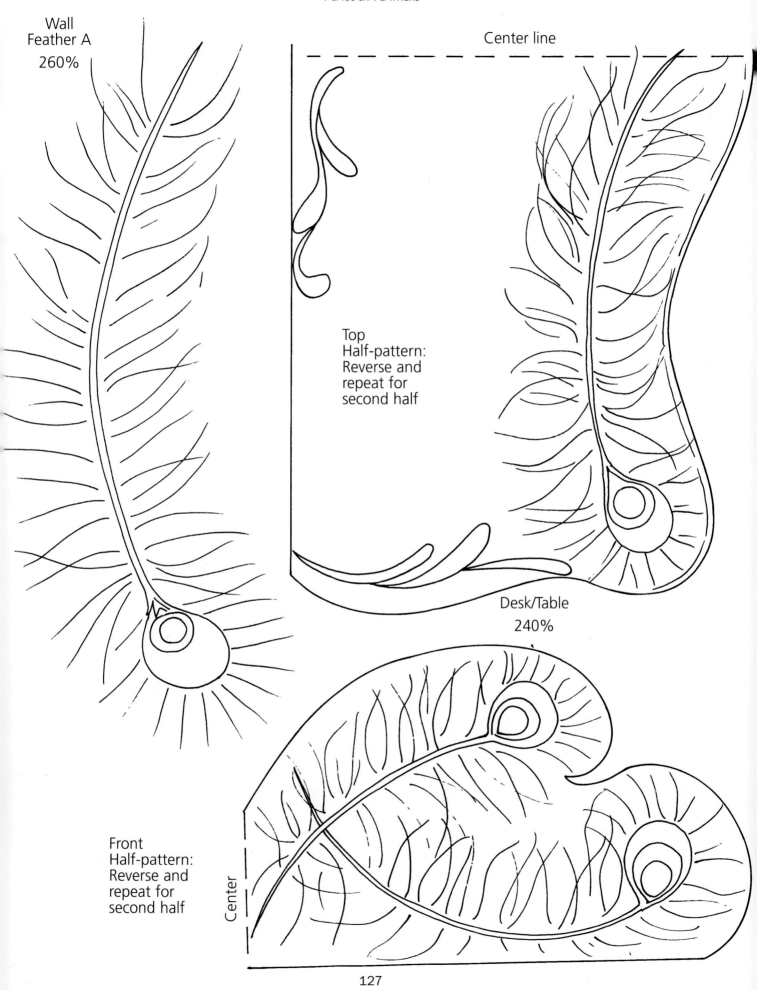

Wall
Feather A
260%

Center line

Top
Half-pattern:
Reverse and
repeat for
second half

Desk/Table
240%

Front
Half-pattern:
Reverse and
repeat for
second half

Center

Enlarge Patterns at % given or to size needed.

Headboard
Scroll Design – 430%
Reverse and repeat
for opposite side.

Center

Add Feather B

Patterns

Mirror – 260%
Repeat around
7" circle

Wall
Feather B
260%

Add Feather A